Coding Mastery

Organize, Maintain, and Optimize

Your Ultimate Guide to Efficient and Sustainable Software Development

Written by:

Sujal Vivek Choudhari

Notice of Copyright

Disclaimer

Table of Contents

Preface

In the ever-evolving world of software development, the ability to manage code effectively is not just a nice-to-have skill—it's a necessity. As a developer, I've witnessed firsthand the challenges that arise from poorly organized codebases, whether it's the frustration of debugging a tangled mess or the inefficiency of maintaining code that no one understands. "Coding Mastery: Organize, Maintain, and Optimize" is my guide to overcoming these challenges, drawn from years of experience and a passion for clean, efficient coding.

This book is for anyone who wants to take their coding skills to the next level, whether you're just starting out or you're an experienced developer looking to refine your practices. Inside, you'll find practical techniques for managing your codebase with clarity and efficiency, from the basics of version control to the advanced strategies of AI-driven code analysis.

Each chapter is designed to be a step-by-step guide to mastering different aspects of code management. You'll learn how to structure your code for maximum readability, how to implement robust testing practices, and how to leverage Agile methodologies for smoother project workflows. We'll also dive into the importance of monitoring your application's performance and ensuring data integrity, as well as the emerging role of AI in code bookkeeping.

But this book isn't just about theory—it's about real-world application. I've included case studies and practical examples to illustrate how these principles can be applied in various development scenarios. By the time you finish reading, you'll have a comprehensive toolkit for organizing, maintaining, and optimizing your codebase, enabling you to deliver high-quality software with confidence.

So, whether you're aiming to streamline your development process, reduce bugs, or simply make your code more enjoyable to work with, "Coding Mastery" is your roadmap to success. Let's dive in and take your coding skills to new heights..

CODING MASTERY
ORGANIZE, MAINTAIN, AND OPTIMIZE

Your Ultimate Guide to Efficient and Sustainable Software Development

Chapter 1

Introduction to Code Bookkeeping

Definition of code bookkeeping

Code bookkeeping refers to the practices and activities that help maintain the organization, readability, and manageability of code in a software development project. It involves tasks that ensure the codebase remains clean, understandable, and efficient over time. While not directly contributing to new functionality, bookkeeping is crucial for the maintainability and scalability of software.

Importance in software development

The importance of bookkeeping cannot be overstated. While formal education often focuses on syntax and logical problem-solving, real-world projects demand a broader set of skills to ensure that code remains understandable and functional over time. It is one thing to write a program that works today; it is another to write one that can be easily read, updated, or extended six months or even years down the line. This is where bookkeeping comes into play—a practice that prioritizes the long-term maintainability of a codebase.

Consider how competitive programmers approach coding platforms like LeetCode. These environments encourage speed and efficiency, which often leads to single-letter variable names and dense, compact code. Similarly, students completing college assignments may squeeze entire projects into a single file, driven by tight deadlines or a lack of guidance on best practices. While these approaches may work for short-term goals, they create significant challenges for maintainability. A programmer revisiting such code later may struggle to decipher its intent, especially when working on larger, more complex projects where clarity is crucial.

Bookkeeping addresses these challenges by emphasizing practices that make codebases easier to understand and work with over time. Clear variable names, modular design, and proper documentation are just some of the habits that help developers stay organized and communicate intent effectively. These habits ensure that the next person—or even the original author, months removed from writing the code—can navigate the project with minimal frustration. This focus on maintainability not only saves time but also reduces errors, making bookkeeping a cornerstone of professional software development.

Challenges of poor code management

Poor code management presents significant challenges in software development, particularly when integrating new team members. A disorganized codebase—often referred to as "spaghetti code" due to its tangled, unstructured nature—can be daunting for newcomers. The lack of clear structure and documentation forces fresh developers to spend excessive time deciphering the code's functionality before contributing effectively. This steep learning curve delays project progress and can lead to frustration and decreased morale among team members.

Debugging becomes a formidable task in poorly managed codebases. When code lacks proper organization and clarity, identifying the root cause of issues is akin to finding a needle in a haystack. This inefficiency not only prolongs the development cycle but also increases the likelihood of introducing new bugs during the troubleshooting process. The absence of systematic code management practices exacerbates these problems, making it difficult to maintain software quality over time.

Modifying or extending poorly managed code is equally challenging. Without a clear understanding of the existing code structure, developers may find themselves rewriting sections of code repeatedly to implement new features or updates. This redundancy leads to wasted effort and can introduce inconsistencies within the codebase, further complicating future maintenance. The cumulative effect is a sluggish development process that struggles to adapt to changing requirements or technological advancements.

Real-world examples highlight the detrimental impact of poor code management. For instance, the Therac-25 radiation therapy machine experienced catastrophic failures due, in part, to software errors stemming from inadequate code management practices. These failures resulted in severe radiation overdoses to patients, underscoring the critical importance of maintaining high-quality code in systems where safety is paramount. (Jamie Lynch, BugSnag)

Neglecting proper code management leads to a cascade of challenges: onboarding new team members becomes time-consuming, debugging is inefficient, and modifying code turns into a monumental task. These issues collectively hinder project progress and can have serious real-world consequences, emphasizing the necessity for diligent code management practices in software development.

Benefits for developers

Effective code management offers numerous benefits that directly address the challenges posed by poorly organized codebases. One significant advantage is the streamlined onboarding process for new team members. When code is well-structured and thoroughly documented, newcomers can quickly grasp its functionality and design, enabling them to contribute more efficiently. This clarity reduces the time and resources typically required for training and acclimation, fostering a more productive development environment.

Robust code management simplifies debugging. With clear version histories and organized code structures, developers can more easily identify and resolve issues. This efficiency not only accelerates the development process but also enhances the overall quality of the software. According to Atlassian, source code management (SCM) tracks a running history of changes to a codebase and helps resolve conflicts when merging updates from multiple contributors.

Well-managed code facilitates easier modifications and updates. Developers can implement new features or make changes without the need to overhaul the entire codebase, saving time and reducing the risk of introducing new errors. Unity emphasizes that SCM allows developers and other stakeholders to see a complete history of all changes made to a shared codebase, ensuring that developers are working with up-to-date code and that there are no conflicting code changes.

Effective code management enhances team collaboration, simplifies debugging, and facilitates easier code modifications, directly addressing the challenges associated with poorly managed codebases.

What will you learn?

Upon completing this book, you will acquire a comprehensive skill set essential for modern software development. You will gain proficiency in version control systems, particularly Git, enabling efficient code management and collaboration. An understanding of code organization principles and modular programming will empower you to structure projects for optimal readability and maintainability.

You will also learn to apply best practices in naming conventions and design principles, such as SOLID, to enhance code clarity and robustness. The book emphasizes the importance of testing, equipping you with the ability to write effective test cases and utilize code coverage metrics to ensure software reliability.

The book covers Agile methodologies, providing insights into iterative development and team collaboration techniques. You will develop debugging skills and understand memory management, crucial for optimizing application performance. The inclusion of topics like application monitoring, crash reporting, and secure coding practices ensures that you are well-versed in maintaining and safeguarding software systems.

By exploring AI integration in code management and sustainable coding practices, you will be prepared to adopt emerging technologies and contribute to environmentally responsible software development. The practical case studies included will offer real-world insights, enabling you to apply learned concepts effectively.

This book aims to transform you into a well-rounded developer who is not only adept at writing code but also proficient in managing, testing, securing, and optimizing software throughout its lifecycle.

Chapter 2

Version Control

Version control systems

Managing multiple versions of a file without a version control system can quickly become chaotic. You might find yourself sifting through files named *draft1.txt, final.txt, final_FINAL.txt,* and *final_FINAL (2).txt,* each representing different iterations of the same document. This approach not only leads to confusion but also increases the risk of overwriting important changes and losing valuable information.

Version control systems (VCS) address these challenges by systematically tracking changes to files over time. With a VCS, you can maintain a clear history of modifications, revert to previous versions when necessary, and collaborate seamlessly with others. This organized method ensures that all changes are documented, reducing the likelihood of errors and enhancing the overall efficiency of your workflow.

By adopting a version control system, you transform the management of your files from a disorganized process into a structured and reliable system, making it easier to track progress, collaborate with others, and maintain the integrity of your work.

Git basics

Git is a versatile tool that streamlines code management, even for those new to version control. With just three fundamental commands—git init, git add, and git commit—you can effectively track changes and maintain a history of your project. This simplicity allows you to focus on development without the complexity of advanced features.

If you a prefer a graphical interface, Git offers desktop applications that eliminate the need for terminal commands, making it accessible to a broader audience.

The core concepts of Git—commits, branches, and merges—are essential for effective code management. Commits capture snapshots of your project at specific points in time, providing a clear history of changes. Branches enable you to work on different features or fixes simultaneously without interfering with the main codebase. Merges allow you to integrate these changes back into the main project seamlessly. These functionalities are fundamental to maintaining an organized and efficient development workflow.

While Git's staging area offers additional control over changes, focusing on commits, branches, and merges provides a solid foundation for effective code management. As you become more comfortable with these basics, you can explore advanced features at your own pace.

Best practices for Git

Implementing a structured Git branching strategy is essential for maintaining an organized and efficient development workflow. A widely adopted approach involves using two primary branches: main and dev.

The main branch serves as the stable version of your project. It should always contain code that is ready for production or sharing with others. To preserve its stability, direct commits to the main branch are discouraged. Instead, all development work should occur in the dev branch. Once features are complete and thoroughly tested in dev, they can be merged into main for release. (Adopt a Git branching strategy, Microsoft Learn)

For larger teams or more complex projects, additional branches can be utilized. Feature branches (feature/) and fix branches (fix/) allow developers to work on specific tasks without affecting the main codebase. These branches are typically merged into dev after completion and testing. This approach ensures that the dev branch remains the primary working branch, integrating all new features and fixes before they are merged into main. (Paulina Ambroziak, Tilburg Science Hub)

By using this branching strategy, you can maintain a clean and manageable repository, facilitate efficient collaboration among team members, and ensure that the main branch always reflects a stable and deployable version of your project.

Branching strategies (e.g., Gitflow)

Gitflow is a branching model that introduces a structured approach to managing code changes, making it particularly beneficial for teams with scheduled release cycles and a need to define a collection of features as a release.

In this model, the main branch serves as the official release history, containing code that is ready for production. The develop branch acts as an integration branch for features, where all completed features are merged and tested before being considered for release. Feature branches are created from develop for individual tasks or features, and once completed, they are merged back into develop. When all planned features have accumulated in the develop branch, a release branch is created for deployments to upper environments. This separation improves control over which changes are moving to which named environment on a defined schedule. (Gitflow branching strategy, AWS)

This structured approach enhances collaboration among team members, ensures that the main branch always reflects a stable and deployable version of the project, and provides a clear path for integrating new features and preparing for releases.

Collaboration workflows (pull requests, code reviews)

In collaborative software development, pull requests and code reviews are essential practices that significantly enhance both code quality and team collaboration. Let's consider an example with Alice, Bob, and Eve. Alice and Bob are working together on a project, and Alice develops a new feature. To ensure that her changes are integrated smoothly, she submits a pull request, essentially proposing her changes to the codebase. This pull request allows Bob and Eve, who is the designated code reviewer, to examine the code before it's merged into the main codebase. Pull requests facilitate parallel development, allowing multiple developers to work on different features without interfering with each other's work. This structure also ensures that all changes are tracked and reviewed, making it easier to follow the evolution of the codebase.

Eve being the reviewer plays a key role in maintaining code quality. She thoroughly checks Alice's changes to ensure they align with coding standards, integrate well with the existing code, and do not introduce new bugs. Eve may suggest improvements or ask for clarification on certain parts, providing Alice with valuable feedback. This process not only helps to improve the quality of the code but also encourages knowledge sharing among team members, promoting a culture of continuous learning and collaboration.

While the practice of using pull requests and conducting code reviews has numerous advantages, there are some potential drawbacks. One of the main challenges is the time investment required for the review process. For larger code changes, reviews can become time-consuming, slowing down the overall development pace. Moreover, if the review is not thorough enough, subtle issues might slip through, which could cause problems down the line. Another challenge is that the process depends on the availability of the reviewer. If Eve is unavailable or overwhelmed with other tasks, it may delay the integration of Alice's changes. Despite these challenges, when executed well, pull requests and code reviews are invaluable tools for ensuring high-quality, maintainable code and fostering collaboration within teams.

Chapter 3

Fundamentals of Code Structure and Organization

Code organization principles

Effective code organization is essential for the long-term maintainability and scalability of any software project. A well-organized codebase allows developers to quickly understand the structure of a project, navigate through it with ease, and collaborate efficiently. One fundamental principle of code organization is modularity, where the code is divided into smaller, self-contained modules or functions that each serve a specific purpose. This approach makes the codebase more manageable and easier to test, as changes to one part of the system have minimal impact on other parts. For instance, a feature or function can be developed independently, making it easier to identify issues and optimize performance.

Another important principle is separation of concerns, which means organizing the code in a way that different aspects of the application are kept distinct. This principle reduces complexity by ensuring that the logic for different tasks—such as handling user input, processing data, and interacting with databases—are isolated from one another. By keeping these concerns separate, developers can work on individual components without worrying about unintentional side effects. For example, the user interface code should be separate from the business logic or data storage code, allowing for cleaner and more understandable code.

Consistency is also a key element in maintaining a well-organized codebase. Using consistent naming conventions, code formatting, and file structures throughout the project ensures that all team members are on the same page. This consistency makes it easier for new developers to join the project, as they can quickly get up to speed with the existing structure. Furthermore, adhering to well-known conventions or design patterns helps reduce ambiguity, as developers can rely on established practices rather than reinventing the wheel for every new project.

By following these code organization principles—modularity, separation of concerns, and consistency—teams can create a codebase that is not only easier to maintain and scale but also more collaborative and adaptable to future changes. These principles lay the groundwork for a cleaner, more efficient development process, making the entire project more manageable and allowing developers to focus on solving problems rather than dealing with cluttered, disorganized code.

Modular programming

Modular programming is a software design technique that involves dividing a program into separate, self-contained modules, each responsible for a specific functionality. This approach enhances code readability, maintainability, and reusability. In Python, this is achieved by creating functions and classes within separate files, known as modules, which can be imported and utilized in other parts of the program.

For example, consider a simple Python program that performs basic arithmetic operations. Instead of writing all the functions in a single file, we can organize them into separate modules.

math_operations.py:

```python
def add(a, b):
    return a + b

def subtract(a, b):
    return a - b
```

main_program.py:

```python
import math_operations

def main():
    x = 10
    y = 5
    sum_result = math_operations.add(x, y)
    diff_result = math_operations.subtract(x, y)
    print(f"The sum of {x} and {y} is {sum_result}")
    print(f"The difference between {x} and {y} is {diff_result}")

if __name__ == "__main__":
    main()
```

In this example, math_operations.py contains functions for addition and subtraction, while main_program.py imports these functions to perform calculations. This separation allows for better organization and easier maintenance.

By adopting modular programming principles, developers can create codebases that are easier to understand, test, and maintain. This approach also facilitates code reuse, as modules can be imported and used across different parts of a program or even in different projects.

For a more in-depth exploration of modular programming in Python, you can refer to the tutorial by **Bernd Klein** on Python Course.

File and folder structure

A well-organized file and folder structure is crucial for the clarity and maintainability of any software project, regardless of the programming language. The primary goal is to create a layout that makes sense for the project's requirements and allows developers to easily find, update, and scale components over time.

The first principle of good file organization is clarity in naming. Files and folders should have meaningful names that reflect their content and purpose. For instance, avoid generic names like file1 or temp, and instead use descriptive names such as user_data, config_settings, or authentication_handler. This ensures that anyone working on the project can immediately identify the file's role within the codebase.

A typical project structure might look something like this:

```
/project_root
    /src             # Source code files
        /module1     # Logic or functionality specific to Module 1
            handler1
            handler2
        /module2     # Logic or functionality specific to Module 2
            processor1
    /docs            # Documentation files
        README.md
    /config          # Configuration files
        settings.cfg
    /assets          # Resources like images, scripts, etc.
        icon.png
        style.css
```

```
/tests                 # Test files
    test_module1
    test_module2
```

The src folder contains the main source code divided into logical modules (e.g., *module1*, *module2*). These modules contain files related to a particular part of the application. The docs folder holds any documentation, including the *README.md* file for project setup, while the config folder stores any configuration settings (e.g., database, environment variables). The assets folder houses external resources, and the tests folder is where the project's unit and integration tests live.

It's important to note that this structure is flexible and can be adjusted to meet the needs of a specific project. For example, larger projects might require additional folders for logs, build artifacts, or scripts, while smaller projects might not need all of these categories. The key is to ensure the structure is intuitive and scalable as the project grows.

By following these principles, you can ensure that your project's file and folder organization remains manageable, clear, and conducive to smooth development and collaboration.

Package management

Package management is an essential practice in software development, especially when you aim to create reusable, plug-and-play components that can be easily integrated into multiple projects. When you create a package, you're essentially turning a piece of code into a standalone unit that can be shared and used across different projects or by other developers. This approach is particularly useful when you want to isolate specific functionality or system components from the rest of the project.

You might consider creating a package when you identify that a certain part of your code is generic enough to be reused in different contexts. For instance, a utility function for data validation, a library for interacting with a database, or a module for managing user authentication can all be packaged as reusable components. This allows you to use the same code in multiple projects without having to rewrite it each time, saving you time and effort.

Packages also help with isolating systems within a project. If your project involves multiple components that are loosely coupled and can function independently, creating packages for each component ensures that they remain modular and maintainable. For example, in a web application, you might have separate packages for user authentication, payment processing, and reporting. By organizing the code into separate packages, you ensure that each part of the system can be developed, tested, and maintained independently.

Creating packages improves collaboration. When the code is packaged, it can be easily shared with other developers or teams. This is particularly beneficial in larger projects or when working in a team environment. Packages can be versioned and managed through package managers, ensuring that everyone uses the correct version of the code, and reducing compatibility issues.

By adopting package management practices, you can ensure that your code remains modular, reusable, and maintainable. It also enables you to build systems that can easily scale as the project grows, without the need for a major restructuring of the entire codebase.

Code documentation

When it comes to documenting your code, timing and approach are key. It's important to not document too early—especially right after writing a piece of code. The reason is simple: your code is likely to change during the development process, and documenting too soon can lead to wasted effort when the code undergoes revisions. Instead, wait until the code has been cleaned up, thoroughly tested, and is stable enough to avoid frequent changes. That's the right time to add documentation.

Instead of relying on single-line comments to explain each part of your code, focus on writing clean, readable code. The best practice is for the code itself to be self-explanatory. If you find yourself adding many comments, it could be a sign that the code isn't as clear as it could be. In such cases, consider refactoring the code for clarity instead of relying on comments. After all, well-written code should communicate its purpose without requiring detailed explanations.

When you do document, focus on explaining when and why a function, class, or module should be used—not what it does. The purpose of the documentation is to provide the necessary context for developers to understand how to use the code effectively. If the "what" of the code is unclear, that's a signal to improve the code itself. Instead, docstrings should focus on usage guidelines, edge cases, and the context in which a function or class should be applied.

Here's an example of how you might document a function properly:

```
def calculate_discount(price, discount_rate):
    """
    Calculates the discount for a given price based on the discount
rate.

    Use this function when the price is a positive number and the
discount rate is between 0 and 1.
    This is particularly useful when applying promotional discounts
in e-commerce applications.
    Arguments:
    price (float): The original price of the product.
    discount_rate (float): The discount rate to apply, expressed as
a decimal (e.g., 0.2 for 20%).

    Returns:
    float: The discounted price after applying the discount.

    Example:
    - calculate_discount(100, 0.2) will return 80.0
    """
    if price < 0 or not (0 <= discount_rate <= 1):
        raise ValueError("Invalid input values.")
    return price - (price * discount_rate)
```

The docstring doesn't explain what the function does—that's clear from the code. Instead, it focuses on when to use the function (valid inputs, such as positive price and discount rate between 0 and 1) and why it's useful (e.g., applying promotional discounts). It also provides a usage example to clarify how the function works in practice.

By focusing on the why and when, your documentation provides value to developers without being redundant. This approach ensures that your code remains clean, and your documentation enhances understanding without over-explaining the obvious.

Chapter 4

Best Practices in Naming Conventions and SOLID Principles

Naming conventions for variables

Naming conventions play a critical role in writing clean, maintainable, and readable code. They help you and your collaborators understand the purpose and scope of variables without diving deep into the logic. Following language-specific conventions is often the best starting point, as these conventions are designed to align with the language's syntax, features, and community practices.

On solo projects, I've found it helpful to enhance standard conventions to improve clarity. For instance, in dynamic languages where types are determined at runtime, I use prefixes like *bool_* or *int_* to indicate a variable's type explicitly. This makes it easier to understand what kind of data the variable is intended to hold, reducing potential errors. Similarly, when dealing with object-oriented programming, I use *m_* as a prefix for private members and *p_* for protected variables, ensuring that the scope and access of the variable are immediately evident.

Constants and defines can stand out when written in uppercase camel case, such as MAX_LIMIT or DEFAULT_TIMEOUT. For function-level variables, I prefer using an underscore prefix (e.g., _temp or _index) to avoid scope ambiguity and to signal that the variable has a limited lifespan. These subtle enhancements bring clarity, especially when the same variable name could appear in different scopes.

Beyond personal preferences, adhering to some universal best practices is beneficial:

- **Descriptive Names:** Variable names should convey their purpose. A name like *totalSales* is far more intuitive than a vague name like x.
- **Avoid Abbreviations:** While brevity is tempting, abbreviations can lead to confusion. Instead of *usrCnt*, write *userCount*—a slightly longer name that's much easier to understand.
- **Consistency:** Stick to one naming style across your project. Whether you choose camelCase, *snake_case*, or *PascalCase*, consistent usage reduces cognitive overhead.
- **Context Clarity:** Variables in different scopes shouldn't have overlapping names that could confuse their purpose. For example, a class-level variable named *userName* shouldn't have a function-level variable with the same name.

Using prefixes, casing, and consistent styles ensures that your code remains readable and scalable. Many language communities, such as Python's PEP 8 and Java's standard practices, offer excellent guidelines. Following these and incorporating your own enhancements as needed can make your code not only functional but also a pleasure to work with.

Readability

Building on the principles of naming conventions, readability is the cornerstone of maintainable and collaborative code. As discussed earlier, clear and descriptive names for variables, classes, and methods play a significant role in ensuring that code is intuitive. This same principle extends beyond individual elements to the broader structure of the codebase itself.

Organizing your codebase so that each class resides in its own file is a natural extension of the clarity achieved through good naming practices. This approach, often referred to as a "*single-class-per-file*" structure, reduces the risk of merge conflicts in collaborative environments. When each file serves a distinct purpose, team members can work independently without worrying about overlapping changes. Additionally, it simplifies navigation, making it easier to locate and understand specific components of the codebase.

Package names and filenames should also adhere to the same clarity standards. A package named *utils.string_operations* clearly conveys its role, whereas a vague name like *module1.submodule2* requires additional effort to decipher. Together, these practices create a cohesive and readable codebase where the purpose of each element is immediately apparent.

Readability isn't just about aesthetics; it's about efficiency. When your codebase is structured to prioritize clarity—both in naming and organization—you save significant time during debugging, onboarding, and even routine development tasks. By consistently applying the principles of clear communication across every aspect of your project, you build software that is approachable, scalable, and a pleasure to maintain.

SOLID principles

The SOLID principles are a set of guidelines for designing robust, scalable, and maintainable software. While they are invaluable in tackling common design issues, it's important not to feel burdened by the need to apply them constantly. Personally, I don't consciously follow SOLID during the initial prototyping phase of a project. In this stage, the primary goal is to get a working solution, regardless of how messy or inefficient the code might be. The focus is on speed and functionality, not perfection. However, whenever I encounter problems in my code—whether it's a design flaw or difficulty in extending functionality—I turn to SOLID principles for solutions.

This reactive approach has worked well for me and can serve as a practical path for beginners. By applying SOLID principles to solve real issues, you develop an intuitive understanding of them over time. With enough practice, these principles will naturally influence your design decisions in future projects, helping you decide effortlessly whether to encapsulate logic in a class, keep it as a function, or refactor for better modularity.

Many developers, including some of my friends, struggle not with logic but with translating that logic into clean, structured code. SOLID principles address this gap by providing a framework for thinking about software design systematically. For those looking to delve deeper, here are the five principles of SOLID:

- **Single Responsibility Principle (SRP):** A class should have one, and only one, reason to change. In other words, each class should handle a single responsibility.
- **Open/Closed Principle (OCP):** Software entities (classes, modules, functions) should be open for extension but closed for modification. This encourages building code that can be extended without altering existing functionality.
- **Liskov Substitution Principle (LSP):** Objects of a superclass should be replaceable with objects of a subclass without altering the correctness of the program. Essentially, derived classes must be substitutable for their base classes.
- **Interface Segregation Principle (ISP):** A client should not be forced to implement interfaces it doesn't use. Large interfaces should be split into smaller, more specific ones.
- **Dependency Inversion Principle (DIP):** High-level modules should not depend on low-level modules; both should depend on abstractions. Additionally, abstractions should not depend on details; details should depend on abstractions.

While it's not necessary to master all these principles at once, practicing them when refactoring or debugging can be immensely beneficial. If you're eager to learn more, tutorials and resources such as "**SOLID Principles Made Easy**" (GeeksforGeeks) or video courses by respected educators like Uncle Bob Martin are great starting points.

"SOLID isn't a rulebook—it's a toolkit."

Use it as needed, and over time, you'll find yourself intuitively crafting better designs with ease.

Design patterns

As a game developer, I have to confess—I've heavily relied on certain design patterns, especially the Singleton pattern. If you've ever wondered what design patterns are, they're essentially tried-and-true solutions to common software design problems. They aren't pieces of code you can copy and paste but rather conceptual blueprints that guide how you structure and organize your code. They help in creating reusable, efficient, and maintainable solutions for recurring issues.

Let me explain the *Singleton pattern* in a context I've often encountered. In Unity game development, I frequently need a class to manage a global game state or control an essential system, such as a sound manager or a game settings handler. Unity's *MonoBehaviour* class is non-static, meaning it can't directly support static methods or properties. This is where the Singleton pattern shines—it ensures that only one instance of the class exists and provides a global point of access to it. This helps avoid redundancy and ensures consistency across the game.

Another pattern I often use is the *Observer pattern*. Imagine an event-driven game system where different objects—players, enemies, and environmental elements—need to react to certain events, such as a player leveling up or time running out. Instead of cluttering the codebase with direct references and calls across various components, the Observer pattern allows objects to subscribe to and unsubscribe from a central event system. While it's powerful, this approach isn't without its challenges; improper handling can lead to circular dependencies and tangled imports, which can quickly spiral into chaos.

Design patterns go far beyond these examples. For instance, the Factory pattern is a staple for creating objects without specifying their exact classes. It promotes flexibility and allows the system to decide which class to instantiate at runtime. The Strategy pattern enables you to switch between different algorithms or behaviors without altering the objects using them—ideal for AI behavior or sorting techniques. Then there's the Adapter pattern, which acts as a bridge between incompatible interfaces, making it invaluable when integrating third-party libraries.

Some patterns lean on fundamental concepts like abstraction and functional interfaces. Abstraction ensures that high-level details remain separated from low-level ones, promoting scalability and simplicity. Functional interfaces, particularly common in modern languages like JavaScript and Python, allow you to pass behavior (functions) as parameters, enabling patterns like Command and Visitor to simplify complex systems.

Design patterns aren't rigid rules—they're flexible tools that can adapt to your specific needs. While you might not use them all, understanding a handful of them can profoundly enhance your ability to write cleaner, more maintainable code. If you're new to design patterns, I recommend exploring books like Design Patterns: Elements of Reusable Object-Oriented Software by the Gang of Four or checking tutorials online. With practice, you'll see patterns emerge in your work naturally, guiding you toward more efficient and elegant solutions.

Code refactoring

I've had mixed experiences. Personally, I've never reused significant chunks of code from previous projects. Why? Because no two projects are exactly the same. Refactoring old code to fit the specific needs of a new project often feels like trying to hammer a square peg into a round hole—it's a mammoth task that rarely yields satisfying results. This is particularly true in fast-moving fields like web development, where new frameworks and paradigms seem to pop up every day. Take, for example, the humorous reality of websites like *dayssincelastjavascriptframework.com*, which inevitably display a big "0." The constant evolution of tools and frameworks makes reusing code from previous projects more trouble than it's worth.

That said, there are exceptions. Some parts of a codebase, especially utility libraries, can be refactored into reusable modules. For example, in game development, creators like **CodeMonkey** have crafted utility packages that they use across projects—and the community benefits from them, too. These packages are designed to address universal needs, such as mathematical calculations or rendering helpers, which don't vary much across projects. In these cases, refactoring the code to generalize functionality makes it reusable and valuable.

So, how should we approach refactoring when it is necessary? The essence of refactoring is improving the internal structure of code without changing its external behavior. Here are some lessons distilled from trusted tutorials and practices:

- **Start Small:** Refactoring doesn't mean rewriting your entire codebase. Start with manageable changes—renaming unclear variables, breaking large functions into smaller ones, or reorganizing classes into cleaner hierarchies.

- **Test as You Go:** Ensure you have a robust set of test cases before refactoring. Without them, you risk introducing subtle bugs while making structural changes. Each step of the refactoring process should maintain the functionality of your code.
- **Eliminate Redundancy:** Look for repeated code patterns and extract them into reusable functions or classes. This practice, called *"DRY" (Don't Repeat Yourself)*, minimizes errors and reduces the effort required to maintain your code.
- **Simplify Complex Code:** If a piece of code is difficult to read or understand, it's likely a candidate for refactoring. Consider using design patterns like Strategy or Factory to make the logic more modular and flexible.
- **Optimize Naming Conventions:** As we've discussed in previous sections, clear and consistent naming conventions can make your refactored code easier to read and maintain.

Refactoring is also an excellent opportunity to revisit your architecture and apply principles like SOLID or DRY, as discussed earlier. If you're interested in diving deeper into refactoring strategies, resources like **Refactoring: Improving the Design of Existing Code by Martin Fowler** or the excellent tutorials on **Refactoring Guru** can provide a wealth of knowledge.

While the decision to refactor code depends on your specific needs, it's a practice that improves maintainability, fosters reusability, and ultimately leads to cleaner and more efficient code. Whether it's adapting an old project for new requirements or crafting a robust utility library, the effort invested in refactoring often pays off in the long run.

Chapter 5

The Importance of Test Cases and Achieving Code Coverage

Test cases definition

Test cases are the building blocks of a robust testing process. Simply put, a test case is a set of specific conditions or inputs, along with expected outcomes, designed to verify that a particular piece of code behaves as intended. Each test case acts like a detective, probing your code to ensure it does exactly what it's supposed to— and nothing it's not. Whether you're testing a login function or a complex algorithm, well-written test cases are your first line of defense against bugs and unexpected behavior.

Types of testing (unit, integration)

There are two main types that you'll frequently encounter: unit testing and integration testing. Both play crucial roles in ensuring your code is functioning as expected, but they serve different purposes. Unit testing focuses on verifying that individual component of your code work correctly in isolation. These are small tests that target specific functions or methods, making sure that each part of your application behaves exactly as it should. Unit testing is essential for catching bugs early and ensures that changes to your code don't break existing functionality. For beginners, it's a good idea to start writing tests for the smallest, most critical pieces of functionality. There are plenty of tools like JUnit, pytest, or Jest to get you started, depending on your programming language of choice.

On the other hand, integration testing checks if different parts of your application work well together. For example, it ensures that when your frontend sends data to your backend, it gets processed correctly, or that data is properly fetched from a database. Unlike unit tests, which focus on isolated pieces, integration tests check the interaction between components. While they may take longer to write and run, they are crucial for catching bugs that might not show up in unit tests. As your project grows, integration tests will help you make sure that everything works cohesively.

For beginners it is generally a good idea to start with unit tests, as they are simpler to write and run. Once you have a good set of unit tests, you can start thinking about integration testing, especially when your application starts interacting with multiple components or external systems. There are plenty of beginner-friendly resources and tools available, like Postman for API testing or Selenium for end-to-end testing, that can guide you as you move into the realm of integration testing.

Writing effective test cases

When it comes to writing test cases, the goal is to ensure that your core logic functions correctly and handles edge cases gracefully. The most effective test cases focus on the critical areas of your code—the parts that are central to the functionality of your application. These are typically the areas that are more prone to subtle errors, like off-by-one mistakes or issues related to error handling. While adhering to proper architecture and writing clean code can greatly minimize syntax errors and misunderstandings of logic, errors in handling special conditions or input are often where things go wrong.

By focusing on testing the core logic, you can catch these subtle bugs before they make it to production. For example, ensure that your code properly handles different types of inputs, including edge cases such as empty strings, null values, or boundary conditions. Testing for these edge cases can often prevent larger issues from arising later in the development process. Additionally, you should test how your application behaves under different failure scenarios, such as incorrect user input or system errors. By anticipating how your system should fail and writing tests around these cases, you ensure that error handling is robust and reliable.

Effective test cases should go beyond simply confirming that your code runs without crashing. They should explore the scenarios where things could go wrong, ensuring that your application handles both expected and unexpected inputs gracefully. The goal is to test your code's ability to handle a variety of situations, catching those elusive bugs that often occur when your program is pushed to its limits.

Code coverage metrics

Code coverage is a critical metric in evaluating the effectiveness of your tests. Simply put, it measures the percentage of your code that is exercised by your test cases. However, it's not just about numbers—code coverage has a direct impact on the reliability and maintainability of your codebase.

> *"If you don't have 100% code coverage, then your tests aren't providing full value."*

This doesn't mean that your tests are useless, but it does mean that there could be areas of your code that are untested, which opens the door for potential bugs.

The goal should always be to test every line of code, ensuring that all paths are covered. While you can't directly check the quality of each individual test just by looking at the coverage percentage, the coverage number itself serves as a useful benchmark for tracking progress. The more coverage you have, the more confident you can be that your code behaves as expected under various conditions. Since many teams and organizations prioritize code coverage as a standard for code quality, maintaining a consistent 100% coverage ensures that your codebase meets the expectations of future developers who will interact with your code.

Yes the quality of your tests matters just as much as the quantity. High coverage is only meaningful if the tests themselves are well-written and address the key logic and edge cases of your code. As the complexity of your code grows, so should the seriousness and depth of your tests. The aim is to not only ensure that every line of code is covered but to also refine and improve the tests as necessary to catch edge cases and critical failures. By striving for 100% code coverage and continuously improving your test suite, you can be confident that your codebase remains stable and reliable, regardless of who takes over the project next.

Continuous integration for testing

Continuous Integration (CI) is an essential practice in modern software development that can drastically improve the quality of your codebase. It revolves around the concept of automatically integrating code changes from multiple developers into a shared repository multiple times a day. The goal is to prevent integration issues that can arise when code changes are merged too infrequently or in large batches. But CI isn't just about integrating code—its primary benefit is its ability to automate testing, ensuring that every change made to your codebase is verified as soon as it's committed.

As we discussed in the previous section about test cases and code coverage, writing tests is only part of the equation. The real power comes from continuously running those tests as soon as new code is introduced. This is where Continuous Integration (CI) really shines. By setting up an automated pipeline that triggers every time code is pushed to the repository, developers ensure that any bugs or issues are caught early. For example, if one developer writes code that breaks a part of the application, the automated CI pipeline will run the entire test suite to detect the issue, alert the developer, and prevent broken code from reaching the main codebase.

What makes CI such a powerful tool for testing is the speed and reliability it offers. Developers can set up CI tools to run their tests on every commit, pull request, or merge. This results in immediate feedback, which drastically reduces the time spent on debugging issues that may not have been noticed until much later in the development process. This real-time feedback loop allows teams to fix problems earlier and more efficiently, ultimately improving the quality of the code and reducing the chances of defects making it to production.

CI pipelines can also enforce best practices for testing. For instance, many CI tools provide built-in features to ensure that tests pass successfully before code can be merged. This creates a system where you don't have to manually check whether your tests have been executed correctly or if they are up-to-date. With CI, you can define testing rules, such as making sure that every push has 100% code coverage, or that only specific tests are triggered based on the changes made.

Another aspect of Continuous Integration that ties into the earlier section about code coverage is the integration of coverage metrics into your CI pipeline. With tools like Coveralls or Codecov, you can easily monitor and track your code coverage trends over time. This means that if your code coverage dips below your required threshold, it will be flagged immediately, preventing low-coverage code from being merged into your codebase. This ensures that your testing practices are always aligned with your quality goals, and that no corner is cut when it comes to test coverage.

Setting up CI tools for your project can vary based on the tools and services you use. Popular CI services like *Travis CI, Jenkins, CircleCI,* and *GitHub Actions* allow you to integrate with your version control system and automate the build, test, and deployment process. Many of these services are highly customizable and provide a range of features like build history, visualizations of test results, and integration with external tools. For example, with *Jenkins*, you can integrate testing tools like *Selenium* for end-to-end testing or *SonarQube* for static code analysis, creating a comprehensive test suite that runs automatically with every code change.

CI also encourages collaboration among developers. Since every code change is tested automatically, developers have a shared responsibility for the stability of the codebase. Issues are identified faster, and developers are more likely to address problems quickly because they know their code will be tested every time they push changes. This collaborative environment leads to higher-quality code overall, as teams adopt a culture of continuous testing and improvement.

As we've seen in earlier sections, writing good tests and achieving code coverage are essential for maintaining a healthy codebase. Continuous Integration takes these practices to the next level by ensuring that testing is always part of the development process. Rather than waiting until the end of a development cycle to run tests, CI offers a continuous flow of testing and feedback that empowers developers to build better, more reliable applications. By integrating testing into the development workflow from the very start, you can ensure that your project remains stable, scalable, and free of critical bugs.

Chapter 6

Agile Development

Agile methodologies overview

Agile development is a concept that revolutionized how software projects are managed and executed. It is not just a set of practices; it is a mindset. In the fast-paced world of software development, the ability to respond quickly to change is crucial, and Agile methodologies facilitate just that. While traditional development methods often follow a linear, waterfall approach, Agile emphasizes flexibility, collaboration, and continuous delivery. The idea is simple: break work into small, manageable chunks, deliver them quickly, and then iterate based on feedback.

When I first encountered Agile, I wasn't exactly a fan. For someone used to working solo or in small teams, the structured and repetitive nature of Agile seemed unnecessary. But over time, especially in team-based or corporate environments, I started to see its value. In larger teams, where multiple developers are working on different aspects of the same product, keeping track of what everyone is doing becomes essential. If you don't have a clear way to track tasks, priorities, and progress, the whole project can easily fall into disarray. That's where Agile's structured methodologies come into play—providing clear guidelines for work management and collaboration.

There is an emphasis on communication and transparency. It's not just about getting the job done—it's about how you work together to get there. The roles in Agile are clearly defined, whether it's the Scrum Master, Product Owner, or the Development Team, everyone has a responsibility in making sure the project moves forward smoothly.

"What you did yesterday or how much code you wrote doesn't matter as much as how well you communicated and collaborated towards the common goal."

In corporate environments, this is a crucial shift because the outcome is often more important than the process. Agile is less about individual contributions and more about the collective effort. While that may not always be my preferred way of working, it is undeniably effective in larger team settings.

Agile focuses on iterative development—something I believe is one of its strongest points. You don't need to worry about delivering the perfect product right out of the gate. Instead, the idea is to release something functional, even if it's not complete, and then keep improving it. This allows you to incorporate user feedback, adjust features, and continuously improve the product without wasting time on features that aren't necessary. Agile isn't about rigidly following a plan; it's about adapting as you go. In many ways, it embraces the idea that failure and mistakes are part of the learning process.

The core of Agile is to create a collaborative environment where feedback is constant, progress is visible, and team members can adapt to changing priorities. As we dive deeper into Agile practices, it becomes clear that these methodologies are not just a project management tool—they are a culture shift. They empower teams to take ownership, make decisions, and adapt to whatever the project throws at them. Whether you are a developer, product owner, or project manager, Agile offers a framework to improve productivity, reduce bottlenecks, and ultimately, create better software. And for me, that's a powerful concept.

Scrum vs. Kanban

Scrum and Kanban are two prominent Agile methodologies, each with distinct approaches to managing work. Scrum operates in fixed-length iterations called sprints, typically lasting two to four weeks, during which a specific set of tasks is completed. This structure includes defined roles such as Scrum Master and Product Owner, and emphasizes regular ceremonies like daily stand-ups and sprint retrospectives. In contrast, Kanban focuses on continuous delivery without fixed iterations. It uses a visual board to track tasks through various stages, allowing for a flexible flow of work and the ability to adapt to changing priorities. Both methodologies aim to enhance efficiency and responsiveness, but they differ in structure and implementation. For a comprehensive comparison, consider exploring resources on **Coursera.**

Iterative development

Iterative development is a software development methodology that emphasizes breaking down the development process into small, manageable cycles called iterations. Each iteration involves planning, design, coding, and testing, resulting in a usable product at the end of each cycle. This approach allows teams to incorporate feedback and make incremental improvements throughout the development lifecycle. (What is Iterative Development?, ITU Online)

For those interested in learning more about iterative development, the **Interaction Design Foundation** offers a comprehensive overview.

Agile planning

Agile development is a methodology that emphasizes flexibility, collaboration, and customer satisfaction. Central to Agile are structured planning and regular meetings, known as ceremonies, which guide the development process. These ceremonies include sprint planning, daily stand-ups, sprint reviews, and sprint retrospectives.

Sprint Planning

At the beginning of each iteration, known as a sprint, the team conducts a sprint planning meeting. During this session, the team selects items from the product backlog to work on, defines the sprint goal, and plans the tasks necessary to achieve that goal. This planning ensures that everyone understands the objectives and the work required.

Daily Stand-ups

To maintain momentum and address any obstacles, the team holds daily stand-up meetings. These brief, typically 15-minute meetings allow each team member to share what they accomplished the previous day, what they plan to work on today, and any challenges they are facing. This practice promotes transparency and quick problem-solving.

Sprint Reviews

At the end of each sprint, the team conducts a sprint review. In this meeting, the team demonstrates the work completed during the sprint to stakeholders, gathers feedback, and discusses any changes or additions to the product backlog. This ensures that the product aligns with stakeholder expectations and allows for adjustments based on feedback.

Sprint Retrospectives

Following the sprint review, the team holds a sprint retrospective. This meeting focuses on the team's internal processes, discussing what went well, what could be improved, and how to implement those improvements in future sprints. The goal is continuous improvement, fostering a culture of learning and adaptation.

These ceremonies are designed to create a structured yet flexible framework that promotes collaboration, transparency, and continuous improvement. By regularly engaging in these practices, teams can adapt to changing requirements, deliver high-quality products, and enhance their development processes over time.

For a more in-depth understanding of Agile planning and its ceremonies, consider exploring resources on **Atlassian's website**.

Agile tools (Jira, Trello)

Agile tools like **Jira** and **Trello** are essential in helping teams implement Agile methodologies efficiently. In earlier sections, we discussed the importance of planning and collaboration in Agile, and tools like these enable teams to stay organized and aligned throughout the process.

Jira, for instance, is widely used in Scrum environments, providing a robust platform for tracking progress, managing sprints, and facilitating communication among team members. It integrates with other tools and offers features like customizable workflows and detailed reporting, making it an excellent choice for teams following more structured Agile practices, such as Scrum.

On the other hand, Trello is a more straightforward tool often preferred by teams using Kanban. It uses a visual board with drag-and-drop features, allowing teams to easily organize tasks and manage their workflow. It's lightweight and user-friendly, which makes it ideal for smaller teams or less complex projects.

Both tools provide a way for teams to visualize and manage their tasks, ensuring that the principles of iterative development and continuous delivery discussed earlier are carried out effectively. For teams looking to dive deeper into Agile tool usage, Atlassian's website and Trello's resources can be valuable starting points.

Chapter 7

Debugging Techniques and Memory Management

Debugging tools

Debugging tools are essential for identifying and fixing issues in your code. As we've discussed earlier, maintaining clean and organized code can minimize the occurrence of bugs. However, even the most structured codebases can run into issues, and that's where debugging tools come in.

Popular tools like *Visual Studio Code's Debugger*, *PyCharm's Debugger*, or even *Chrome Developer Tools* for web development help you identify bugs quickly and efficiently. These tools provide features like variable inspection, call stack views, and console outputs, making it easier to track down where and why a bug is occurring.

When you run your code in these debugging environments, you can see real-time changes to your variables and identify problematic lines, reducing the trial-and-error process. This was something we highlighted in earlier chapters, where keeping your code clean helps make debugging smoother.

Whether you are developing a web application or a game, integrating these tools into your workflow helps you streamline the debugging process and catch issues early. The key takeaway is that debugging is not just about finding bugs—it's about creating an environment where you can identify and fix issues quickly, ensuring your code runs as smoothly as possible.

Breakpoints

I remember the first time I learned about breakpoints—it was like magic. I had always been used to running my code and fixing errors as they appeared, but when I realized I could pause my code at a specific line and see how everything was changing, I was hooked. It was a whole new level of control.

A breakpoint allows you to stop the execution of your code at a certain point, enabling you to inspect variables, the call stack, and the flow of your program up to that moment. This step-by-step approach helps catch issues that might be harder to find in larger codebases, allowing you to understand the state of your program at any given time.

Just like we discussed earlier in modular programming and code organization, breakpoints help make it easier to spot issues and track the flow of your program—whether it's catching an unexpected change in a variable or tracking down an elusive bug. It's an incredibly powerful tool for improving the debugging process and gives you a clearer view of how your code behaves.

Step-by-step execution

Step-by-step execution is one of the most powerful techniques in debugging, allowing you to go through your code line by line. This approach helps you understand how your code is executing and pinpoint where things are going wrong.

When you encounter a bug, it's easy to get overwhelmed by the sheer number of lines in your code. Instead of trying to figure out where things went wrong in the whole program, step-by-step execution allows you to break the process down. You can pause the execution at each line to inspect how data changes, track the flow of control, and see if certain functions or conditions are working as expected.

Let us consider an example, when debugging a function, you can step into it to see how its logic is carried out. If there's an issue, you can pinpoint the exact line where things go awry instead of sifting through the entire codebase.

This method also helps you understand how different parts of your program interact with each other. It's like watching the puzzle pieces come together, allowing you to identify mismatched or missing pieces that could be causing errors.

Just as we have talked about good code organization and how breaking code into smaller pieces can make debugging easier, step-by-step execution complements this by letting you follow the code's flow precisely. Whether you're working with smaller scripts or large systems, this debugging technique helps you slow down the process and give each part of your code the attention it needs, making it much easier to fix errors.

Memory leaks detection

Memory leaks can be a developer's worst nightmare, and I remember the good ol' days when I'd watch a loop run endlessly, with memory usage rising steadily without any sign of stopping. It's one of those bugs that's hard to spot at first, but once you notice it, you can't unsee it. The memory usage climbs, and the application starts to slow down, but the cause seems elusive until you start digging into the details.

With modern debuggers, you can track memory usage in real-time, which makes identifying and fixing memory leaks much easier. By inspecting variables, you can see where the memory is being allocated and whether it's being properly released when it's no longer needed. In fact, some debuggers even let you inspect the very memory locations where variables are stored, allowing you to detect if something is hogging memory unnecessarily.

As we discussed earlier in debugging tools and step-by-step execution, having that kind of insight into your code is invaluable. With memory leaks, it's not just about inspecting the code's flow but about identifying patterns that lead to excessive memory usage. Are you allocating memory in a loop and never freeing it? Is a variable holding onto memory when it should have been cleared? These are the kinds of issues that debuggers help you catch.

Detecting memory leaks early on ensures your application remains efficient and doesn't suffer from performance degradation over time. It's all part of keeping your code healthy and avoiding the types of issues that can drain resources, which we've touched on throughout the book, from code organization to profiling for performance optimization.

Garbage collection in Java/Python

When I think about memory management issues, I often rant about memory leaks, but there's a solution, right? Well, thankfully, in *Java, Python,* and even *Rust,* garbage collection has been implemented to handle memory management automatically. You don't have to worry about manually deallocating memory, as these languages take care of that for you. This is in contrast to languages like C and C++, where you need to manage memory explicitly, and the risk of memory leaks is far greater.

Of course, I'll admit, C++ still holds a special place in my heart. There's something about the low-level control it gives you that's hard to let go of. But when it comes to tackling memory leaks, I can't deny the benefits of a language with garbage collection built-in. Java's and Python's automatic garbage collection systems track objects that are no longer in use and automatically free up memory, so you don't have to worry about memory being wasted on objects that no longer serve a purpose.

In Java, the *Garbage Collector* (GC) does this work in the background, reclaiming memory by removing unused objects from memory. You don't have to worry about freeing objects yourself—it's done automatically, although there are times when you can fine-tune the GC behavior based on your app's requirements. Python follows a similar approach with its own garbage collection mechanism, relying on reference counting to track objects and remove them when no longer referenced. The *Python GC* further assists by identifying objects involved in circular references and cleaning them up.

As we discussed in the previous section on memory leaks detection, with the power of garbage collection, you get to avoid those kinds of issues altogether. The system itself manages memory efficiently, allowing you to focus more on your code logic rather than the ins and outs of manual memory management. However, this doesn't mean the problem is completely gone—garbage collection can only do so much. Understanding how it works and when it's triggered can still help you optimize your code to prevent memory bottlenecks.

So, while I will always have a soft spot for C++ and its manual approach to memory management, I can definitely appreciate the convenience and safety that languages with garbage collection bring to the table.

Profiling for performance optimization

When it comes to optimizing performance, profiling is one of the most essential techniques to identify bottlenecks in your code. Personally, I've spent quite a bit of time using the Unity Profiler to pinpoint performance issues in my games. It's amazing how you can see exactly where your code is lagging, whether it's in terms of CPU usage, memory allocation, or rendering. The profiler shows you how long each function takes to execute, where memory is being consumed, and where things can be streamlined.

The great thing about profiling tools is that they are not exclusive to Unity. Other development environments offer similar features to help you optimize your code. Python has *cProfile*, which provides a detailed report on where time is spent in your code. Java also has a variety of profiling tools like *VisualVM* or *JProfiler* to track down performance issues, whether it's CPU usage, memory consumption, or thread activity.

What profiling essentially does is break down your program's behavior and helps you see which parts are inefficient or consuming too many resources. This insight allows you to focus your optimization efforts on the areas that matter most, instead of guessing or making blind changes. For example, if you discover that a certain function is taking way longer to execute than expected, you can dig deeper into it and identify whether it's due to an algorithmic issue, excessive memory allocation, or another factor.

Profiling isn't about blindly speeding up everything in your code; it's about understanding what's actually slowing you down and then making targeted changes to address those specific problems. So, whether you're working in Unity, Python, Java, or any other language, profiling tools can help you track down performance bottlenecks and optimize your code efficiently. It's an invaluable skill to have in your toolbox if you want to write performant, scalable software.

Chapter 8

Monitoring Applications and Crash Reporting

Application performance monitoring (APM)

Imagine you've just released your game to thousands of players. The excitement is palpable, and you can't wait to see how they respond. But suddenly, players start reporting that the game freezes during a certain level, or the frame rate drops so low it's unplayable. You panic, don't you? After all, you've tested the game thoroughly, or so you thought. But how could you fix this if you don't know what's causing the issue?

This is where Application Performance Monitoring (APM) comes in. APM is like a trusty sidekick—always watching over your application's health and performance in real-time, catching problems before they explode into full-scale disasters. In my own experience working in game development, APM tools saved me from many nights of sleepless worry, especially when working on large multiplayer games where performance bottlenecks could easily ruin the player experience. If you don't monitor your app's performance in real-time, you may only catch issues after players have already encountered them, leading to bad reviews and a tarnished reputation.

APM is a sophisticated system of tools designed to track the performance of your application, ensuring that all components— like the backend servers, the database, the front-end interface, or even the code itself—are running smoothly. With APM, you can quickly pinpoint performance bottlenecks, memory leaks, high response times, and even failed transactions. It's not just about seeing if the app crashes (although, that's also important); it's about catching performance issues early, before they become noticeable to users.

Let me tell you about a time when we were developing a large-scale mobile game, and our APM tool literally saved the release. We were working with a live service that had real-time multiplayer matches. The last thing we wanted was players getting kicked out of matches or experiencing lag. So, we set up an APM system to monitor things like server response time, network latency, and error rates. One afternoon, the APM system alerted us that a specific API call was taking much longer than it should. The tool provided detailed insights into the request chain, pinpointing exactly where the delay occurred. We were able to fix it before the players even noticed!

Also, in web development APM can be equally important. Take for example an e-commerce site. It's crucial to ensure that pages load quickly, the checkout process is smooth, and user transactions don't fail. If one of these processes is delayed, you could lose revenue. With APM, you can see if there are any parts of the website that are slowing down or causing errors, like a poorly optimized image or a slow database query.

There are several popular APM tools out there, each with its own strengths. *New Relic* is a well-known tool in the industry that helps developers track server performance and pinpoint slow transactions. It provides comprehensive data, from the database queries to the application layer. *Datadog* is another great tool that not only tracks performance metrics but also integrates with other systems, such as cloud monitoring and network tracking. For those working on cloud-based applications, tools like **AWS CloudWatch** and **Azure Application Insights** offer fantastic features to monitor cloud services in real-time.

But APM isn't just about tracking metrics. It's about actionable insights. It's about getting data that leads to real fixes, rather than just knowing there's a problem. It's about ensuring a seamless user experience, no matter how complex your application is. The best APM tools provide user-friendly dashboards with clear, digestible data so developers can focus on what needs to be done instead of sifting through log files. You want to know which function is consuming too much CPU, or which API is failing—APM provides that in seconds.

APM is a vital tool for any serious software developer or team. Without it, you're flying blind, hoping nothing breaks in production. But with it, you can monitor performance 24/7, catch potential issues early, and ensure your users have the best experience possible. Trust me—whether you're building games, websites, or mobile apps, APM is like your own personal health check-up system for your software. And as with health, it's always better to monitor than to wait for a breakdown!

Crash reporting systems

Crashes are a frustrating but inevitable part of software development. Whether it's a mobile app or a game, no matter how much testing we do or how robust the code seems, unexpected crashes are bound to happen. The real challenge is detecting these crashes swiftly, gathering the relevant data, and ensuring that the development team can act on it efficiently. This is where crash reporting systems come into play.

Think about a scenario in a game development project. You're building a new feature, and everything seems fine during development and initial testing. However, once the game reaches your players, you begin to hear reports of crashes during certain in-game events. This is where a good crash reporting system will save the day. A robust crash reporting system will help you track those crashes, collect necessary information, and give you a clear path to diagnosing and resolving the issue.

A custom crash reporting system gives you full control over the crash detection process. Instead of relying on default tools that may collect too much or too little information, you can gather precisely what you need for your specific project. Whether it's a game, a mobile app, or a web application, you'll need to know what the user was doing when the crash occurred, what device they were using, the app's state, and any specific error messages or logs that might shed light on the issue.

Implementing a crash reporting system doesn't require complex tools or frameworks. You can create your own lightweight version, depending on the needs of your project. Typically, the process starts with a try/catch block, which wraps the critical parts of your application where crashes are most likely to happen. When an exception is thrown, the catch block is triggered, and the system can log the exception, gather the relevant details, and send the crash data to a server for analysis.

Let's imagine this in pseudo code. Here's a simplified version of how such a system might look:

```
function main():
    try:
        runApplication()  // This is where your app's core logic runs
    catch(exception):
        handleCrash(exception)

function handleCrash(exception):
    crashReport = createCrashReport(exception)
    crashReport.addDetails(getStackTrace())
    crashReport.addDetails(getDeviceInfo())
    crashReport.addDetails(getAppVersion())
    crashReport.addDetails(getTimestamp())

    if isNetworkAvailable():
        sendCrashReportToServer(crashReport)
    else:
        storeCrashReportLocally(crashReport)

function createCrashReport(exception):
    report = new CrashReport()
    report.message = exception.message
    return report
```

In this scenario, your main function runs the application. If any part of the application throws an exception (a crash), the exception is caught in the catch block, and the *handleCrash()* function is called. This function then creates a detailed crash report that includes information such as the error message, the stack trace, device details, app version, and the timestamp of the crash.

Once the crash report is generated, the system checks whether there's an internet connection. If the network is available, it sends the crash report to the server where it can be logged and analyzed. If the network is unavailable, the report is stored locally on the device so it can be sent later when the user reconnects.

The main benefit of using a custom crash reporting system like this is that it allows you to gather critical crash data in a format that's specific to your app's needs. For example, in a game, it could be extremely helpful to know which in-game event triggered the crash or what level the player was on when the app crashed. These details allow you to focus on the most important issues, prioritize fixes, and track recurring problems across different devices and app versions.

In addition to logging crash reports, it's a good idea to include as much relevant contextual information as possible. For instance, if the crash happened during a specific user action (like tapping a button or completing a level), this information can help your team reproduce the crash and debug it more effectively. Including device-specific data such as OS version, memory usage, and hardware details can also provide more context to pinpoint the issue.

One thing to keep in mind is that crash reports can be incredibly valuable for improving your app's stability and user experience, but you need to strike a balance. Too much data can overwhelm your server or database, while too little data can leave you with gaps that make debugging difficult. By collecting the right amount of information—such as the error message, stack trace, device info, and app version—you can ensure that your team has the necessary context to fix the issue.

Lastly, this kind of system should ideally be scalable. As your app grows and you push new versions to users, the volume of crash reports can increase. You'll need to have a system in place that can handle large amounts of incoming crash data, categorize it, and help prioritize the issues that need attention first.

Error logging best practices

When it comes to error logging, consistency and clarity are paramount. Developers often overlook how crucial it is to have robust and structured logging in place. Without proper error logs, debugging can feel like looking for a needle in a haystack. As you grow in your development journey, you'll start realizing that having accurate and consistent logs can save you hours, if not days, of debugging time.

One tool I personally use and highly recommend is *TraceBook*, a logging utility I developed that automatically tracks function parameters and return types, streamlining the process of error tracking. When you use *TraceBook*, you don't have to manually log each parameter or function return; it handles all of that for you, allowing you to focus on the actual logic of your code.

To implement *TraceBook*, all you need is to install the package, and the rest is taken care of. In any function you want to track, *TraceBook* automatically logs the parameters and return values, making it easier to trace any issues that may arise. The best part is that it keeps everything organized and easy to access, so even if you're working on larger projects, you won't get lost in a sea of logs.

Plus, *TraceBook* helps reduce human error—no more forgetting to log crucial information that could have pointed out the issue much earlier.

The documentation is simple, so once you install the package, you can get started in no time. You can check out the details on the *PyPI* page or explore the GitHub repository if you want to dive deeper into how it works. Even for beginners, using *TraceBook* provides a gentle introduction to automatic logging without needing to worry about manually handling all those details.

Real-time monitoring tools

Real-time monitoring tools are indispensable for maintaining the health of any application. Imagine a system running in production, and something goes wrong. Without a real-time monitoring solution in place, it can take hours, if not days, before the issue is detected and addressed. That delay could lead to service downtime, loss of user trust, and ultimately, a financial impact. This is where real-time monitoring tools come in.

These tools provide continuous oversight of your application, tracking performance metrics, error rates, user activity, and much more. The main goal is to ensure that you catch issues as they happen, or even better, before they affect the end user. For instance, if a user tries to access a specific page and the server takes too long to respond, a real-time monitoring tool will raise an alert, giving the development team the information they need to act quickly.

Many of these tools also provide visualizations and dashboards that show key performance indicators (KPIs), such as response times, server load, error rates, and traffic patterns. These dashboards make it easy to identify trends, spot performance bottlenecks, and see how your application is behaving in real time.

Real-time monitoring is not just about identifying issues but also about being proactive. By consistently monitoring, you gain insights into how your system performs under different conditions, helping you fine-tune it for optimal performance. Some popular tools in this space include Prometheus, Grafana, Datadog, and New Relic. Each tool offers a different approach to monitoring, from infrastructure metrics to user interactions and application performance, giving developers a well-rounded view of how their application is functioning in real-time.

Performance dashboards

Performance dashboards are critical for monitoring the health and efficiency of an application or system in real time. While I personally never found the need to build such dashboards—mainly because I've worked with teams that focused primarily on the coding side, leaving the monitoring and dashboarding to specialized roles or teams—many developers will find that performance dashboards are invaluable for gaining actionable insights into how their application is performing in production.

A performance dashboard serves as a visual representation of key metrics that help you understand how your application is behaving under load, how well it's meeting its service-level objectives, and if there are any immediate issues that need attention. These metrics typically include response times, throughput, error rates, resource utilization (CPU, memory, disk), and user activity. A good dashboard provides a centralized location where anyone involved in managing the system—from developers to operations teams—can get an at-a-glance view of the most important data.

For developers, these dashboards can act as an early warning system for performance bottlenecks, such as slow database queries, high response times, or even the number of failed API calls. By having these metrics displayed in a clear and concise way, developers can address issues before they affect the user experience.

Many real-time monitoring tools, like Prometheus, Grafana, Datadog, and New Relic, offer customizable performance dashboards that allow you to pull in data from various sources and visualize it in real-time. Grafana, for instance, is well-known for its flexibility and ability to integrate with many different data sources, including databases, cloud services, and more, providing powerful visualizations that help you spot trends and anomalies.

These dashboards can be fine-tuned to meet specific needs, whether that's tracking response times for a certain set of endpoints, monitoring CPU usage over time, or keeping tabs on server uptime. The goal is to get real-time insights that help you maintain optimal performance and quickly identify any problems that might crop up.

Chapter 9

Tracking Usage and Ensuring Data Integrity

User activity tracking

Tracking user activity is essential in understanding how users interact with your application, whether it's a web app or a standalone software product. By capturing and analyzing these interactions, you can gain valuable insights into the functionality that users engage with most, detect usage patterns, and even identify pain points where users might be encountering issues.

In the context of web applications, tracking user activity typically involves using tools like *Google Analytics, Mixpanel*, or custom logging systems that track page views, button clicks, form submissions, etc. These tools offer easy integration into web applications and can capture a variety of user actions. For instance, you could track how long a user spends on a particular page, what they click on, what they search for, and whether they encounter any errors. This information can be stored in a database or external analytics tool, and can even be aggregated to show overall usage statistics, popular features, and engagement trends.

When it comes to standalone applications, the process of tracking user activity becomes more nuanced. In desktop or mobile applications, you can still track user actions, but you need to implement a more manual logging system. Let's imagine you are developing a standalone desktop app. In this case, tracking user activity can involve recording interactions with the user interface (UI), such as opening specific windows, clicking buttons, or performing certain tasks. You can set up event listeners to log these activities and store them locally or send them to a central server.

For example, consider an app that tracks when a user opens a file or saves a document. You could log the file name, timestamp, and the action (open/save). Similarly, for more complex software like games, you could track events like game level progression, item usage, or achievement unlocking. Each of these actions can give you insight into how users engage with your software. Here is a brief pseudocode representation of tracking a user's file open event in a standalone desktop application:

```
// Pseudo code for logging user activity in a standalone application
function logUserActivity(activityType, activityDetails) {
    // Get current timestamp
    timestamp = getCurrentTimestamp()

    // Create an event object to store activity details
    event = {
        "activity_type": activityType,
        "details": activityDetails,
        "timestamp": timestamp
    }

    // Save event locally or send to server
    storeEvent(event)
}

// Example: Logging file open activity
logUserActivity("file_open", {"file_name": "example.txt"})
```

This example highlights how to record a basic user activity. You can expand on this by including more details, such as the user's operating system version, app version, and more, depending on what's relevant for your application.

A key consideration when tracking user activity, especially in non-web applications, is privacy. In the context of legal compliance, it's important to balance the need for data with users' rights. This means you should be transparent with your users about what data is being collected, how it will be used, and ensure that it is stored securely. For example, tracking user actions like opening files or logging into a system should be limited to non-sensitive data unless explicitly stated otherwise in your privacy policy.

You should be careful not to over-collect data. Avoid tracking highly sensitive information such as passwords, financial information, or personally identifiable details (PII) unless absolutely necessary. Non-sensitive data, such as the features the user interacts with, timestamps of actions, and device specifications, can still provide valuable insights into user behavior without violating privacy concerns.

Some of the common types of user activity data to track in a non-web application include:

- **User actions:** Which buttons were pressed, what menus were selected, and what actions the user took.
- **Session duration:** How long the user spends on a particular task or in a specific part of the application.
- **Error occurrences:** Tracking when a user encounters an error (e.g., app crashes or exceptions) can help you identify and address bugs.
- **Feature usage:** Which features are used most often, and which features might be underutilized or ignored.

- **User behavior flow:** Understanding the sequence of actions users take in the app, such as the paths users follow from one screen to another, can help refine the user experience.

Usage analytics

Collecting usage analytics is crucial for understanding how your application is performing in real-world conditions and how users are interacting with it. In previous sections, we discussed tracking user activity, which serves as a foundation for gathering meaningful usage data. By monitoring and analyzing usage patterns, you gain insights that help you make informed decisions about future improvements, feature prioritization, and user experience enhancements.

From a high-level perspective, usage analytics allow you to see what parts of your application are being used most frequently and which features might be underutilized or causing issues. For example, if you notice that a specific feature is hardly ever used, it could indicate that it's either not meeting users' needs or it's buried too deep in the UI to be easily discovered. Conversely, if a feature is heavily used, you can further optimize it or build additional functionality around it to enhance user satisfaction.

But it's not just about the features. Usage analytics also help you identify bottlenecks in your application, where users may be experiencing delays or difficulties. For instance, if users repeatedly abandon a certain action or process, this could signal a usability problem, performance issue, or a poorly designed workflow. In web applications, tools like *Google Analytics or Mixpanel* provide insights into how users flow through your site, which pages they visit, how long they stay, and where they drop off. With this data, you can adjust your application to remove friction points and improve the overall user journey.

For standalone applications, usage analytics can be even more crucial because they allow you to capture valuable information about app performance, error occurrences, and user behavior on various devices. For example, in game development, you can track user progression, achievement unlocking, or in-app purchases, and use this information to adjust difficulty levels or design new content. The ability to understand how users are interacting with your software outside of controlled environments helps you optimize and improve performance, ultimately creating a better user experience.

As we've touched upon before, legal and ethical considerations are important when collecting usage data. It's essential to be transparent with your users and ensure that only non-sensitive information is gathered unless explicitly permitted. This aligns with earlier discussions on user activity tracking, where we noted that over-collection of data can infringe on privacy. By collecting only the data that truly matters for improving your product, and respecting users' privacy preferences, you can maintain their trust while still gaining valuable insights.

Usage analytics provide actionable data that helps you identify user behaviors, optimize features, and fine-tune your application. By using this data responsibly, you can deliver a product that not only meets but exceeds user expectations.

Data validation techniques

Data validation techniques are essential for ensuring that the data collected and processed by your application is accurate, consistent, and meets the expected format. Without proper validation, you risk introducing errors, inconsistencies, or security vulnerabilities into your system, which can lead to unexpected behaviors or even data corruption.

Data validation can be broken down into a few key aspects:

- **Type Checking:** Ensuring that the data provided by users or external sources matches the expected type (e.g., integer, string, boolean). This helps avoid issues where, for example, a user inputs text when a number is expected.
- **Format Validation:** Ensuring that data follows the correct format. For instance, an email address should follow the pattern name@domain.com. Similarly, dates should follow a standardized format, like YYYY-MM-DD.
- **Range and Boundaries Checking:** Ensuring that numerical or date values are within a valid range. For example, validating that a user's age is a positive integer and falls within a reasonable range (e.g., 0 to 120).
- **Cross-field Validation:** This involves validating that values in one field are consistent with other fields in the same form or dataset. For instance, if a user is creating an account and inputs their password and a confirmation password, you need to check that both passwords match.
- **Sanitization:** Cleaning and removing any unwanted or dangerous characters in the input data, particularly in web applications, to avoid vulnerabilities like SQL injection or cross-site scripting (XSS).

Validating data should happen at multiple points: on the client side (in the browser or application before submitting), on the server side (to catch invalid data that bypasses client validation), and within your database (to ensure the integrity of stored data).

Data consistency

Data consistency is crucial to ensure that the data in your system remains accurate, reliable, and synchronized across various parts of your application. When data isn't validated properly, inconsistencies arise, leading to issues such as conflicting values, errors, and unreliable reports.

By validating data, you enforce rules that ensure consistency, making it easier to store and manage data in databases or data warehouses. Consistent data ensures that each entry is uniform and predictable, which is vital for generating accurate reports, making data-driven decisions, and maintaining system integrity. It also helps in preventing redundant or conflicting data, which can make future queries and analytics smoother and more reliable.

Data consistency also plays a key role in scalability. As data grows, maintaining consistency becomes even more critical, especially when integrating data from multiple sources. Validating data from the start sets a solid foundation for building a stable and efficient system.

Encryption for data security

Encryption is the process of encoding data so that only authorized parties can access it. This is particularly crucial when dealing with sensitive information, such as personal user data or software credentials, as it prevents unauthorized access during transmission or while stored in databases. Without proper encryption, sensitive data is vulnerable to interception, theft, or misuse by malicious actors.

When discussing encryption for data security, Transport Layer Security (TLS) is one of the most widely used and best methods to secure data in transit. It ensures that the data being transferred over the internet, such as between a user's browser and a web server, is encrypted, maintaining confidentiality and integrity. TLS protects against eavesdropping, tampering, and forgery, and it is essential for securing sensitive transactions, like online banking or e-commerce.

For data at rest, Advanced Encryption Standard (AES) is considered one of the most secure encryption algorithms. AES ensures that the stored data, whether in databases or on cloud servers, remains protected from unauthorized access. AES encryption can be implemented with varying key lengths (128, 192, or 256 bits), with the higher key lengths offering increased security.

While encrypting data is necessary, managing encryption keys is just as important. Proper key management ensures that encryption remains secure, preventing unauthorized parties from accessing or decrypting the protected data. Tools like *HashiCorp Vault or AWS Key Management Service (KMS)* can assist in securely storing and managing encryption keys.

By adopting these best practices, you ensure that sensitive data—whether in transit or at rest—remains secure, thus protecting both users and your application.

For further learning, you can explore resources like **OWASP (Open Web Application Security Project)** for more insights on secure encryption techniques.

Case Studies of GDPR Non-compliance

Let's take a look at a few significant cases where GDPR non-compliance led to hefty fines, legal battles, and public scrutiny. These cases underscore the importance of handling personal data correctly to avoid legal ramifications.

Meta's €1.2 Billion Fine

In 2023, *Meta* (formerly Facebook) found itself in hot water when the *Irish Data Protection Commission* (DPC) slapped them with a record-breaking **€1.2 billion fine**. This happened because Meta had been transferring personal data of EU citizens to the United States without ensuring adequate data protection. The case highlights the crucial aspect of data transfers outside the EU, which we discussed earlier regarding data security and the importance of legal safeguards. The ruling emphasized that any such transfer without proper mechanisms—such as Standard Contractual Clauses (SCCs)—is a violation of GDPR.

This brings us back to one of the core concepts we discussed before: the importance of encryption and securely managing data in transit. The ruling made it clear that data transfer outside the EU should not bypass essential privacy standards. So, always ensure that data being transferred across borders complies with the right data protection clauses to avoid penalties (edpb.europa.eu).

The Schrems II Judgment

Speaking of cross-border data transfers, let's look at the *Schrems II* case from 2020. The *Court of Justice of the European Union* (CJEU) ruled that the EU-U.S. *Privacy Shield*, which many companies relied on to transfer personal data between the EU and U.S., was invalid. This judgment was significant because it disrupted how companies handled international data transfers and underscored the need for appropriate safeguards when transferring personal data beyond the EU.

This ruling ties directly into our earlier discussion about compliance and the legalities of transferring user data. If you're transferring data internationally, the Schrems II case is a reminder that you need more than just a simple agreement—you need assurances that the data is handled in a way that meets EU standards. To ensure your organization doesn't fall into the same trap, look into alternatives like SCCs or Binding Corporate Rules (BCRs) (reuters.com).

EU vs. The European Commission

This case was interesting because it saw the EU's own institutions in court over data protection violations. In 2025, the EU General Court ruled that the European Commission was responsible for mishandling data and must compensate a German citizen for violating their own laws. Even the European Commission, which sets regulations, found itself on the wrong side of GDPR compliance when it failed to protect personal data properly.

For those working in large organizations or governmental bodies, this case is a wake-up call. It shows that GDPR applies universally, even to the entities that enforce it. So, whether you are part of a small startup or a large corporation, understanding and implementing GDPR is non-negotiable (reuters.com).

How to Avoid Legal Consequences

In light of these cases, we can draw several conclusions on how to avoid facing such issues. First and foremost, it's essential to understand that GDPR compliance is about more than ticking boxes. It's about ensuring that data is handled securely, transparently, and with respect for user rights. Here are some best practices for compliance:

Get Explicit Consent

As we discussed earlier, obtaining informed consent is key. Ensure that users clearly agree to the processing of their data, with options to manage or withdraw consent at any time. This isn't just best practice—it's a legal requirement under GDPR.

Ensure Secure Data Transfers

If you're handling cross-border data transfers, make sure you're using mechanisms that meet GDPR's standards, like Standard Contractual Clauses (SCCs) or Binding Corporate Rules (BCRs), especially after the Schrems II case.

Regular Data Audits

Conducting regular audits of your data processing practices can help you identify potential vulnerabilities or violations early. This proactive approach can save you from facing heavy fines down the line.

By following these steps, you can keep your organization on the right side of the law while protecting your users' data. Ultimately, respecting GDPR isn't just about avoiding penalties—it's about building trust with your users and ensuring they feel safe using your product or service.

Chapter 10

Task Management with Kanban and Other Tools

Kanban boards

Kanban boards are an incredibly useful tool for organizing tasks and maintaining a clear overview of a project's progress. In my experience, I've used Kanban for game development projects and even during long hackathons like SIH. The key benefit of Kanban is that it helps you visualize the flow of tasks, making it easier to know exactly who is working on what and the status of different tasks.

However, it's important to note that Kanban boards are only effective if the team regularly updates them. Without updates, the board can quickly become outdated and lose its usefulness. It's like keeping track of commits in Git — if the team isn't consistently pushing their changes, the repository isn't going to reflect the true state of the project.

If you've already read through earlier sections on Agile tools, you'll find that Kanban integrates seamlessly with project management tools like Jira or Trello. These tools allow for easy tracking and managing of tasks, and they offer the flexibility to adapt Kanban practices to your team's workflow.

Task prioritization

When it comes to task prioritization, the key is to focus on what matters most for the success of your project. From my perspective, the *Minimum Viable Product* (MVP) is the most crucial thing to prioritize. The MVP is the simplest version of your product that still delivers value to your users. It should contain only the core features necessary to solve the problem at hand. Getting the MVP ready quickly ensures that you can validate your product idea, gather feedback, and adjust before investing too much time in features that may not matter.

For instance, in a game development project, if you're building a platformer, the MVP might just include the character, basic movement, and one or two levels. These core mechanics should be ready within the first week of work. Once these are working, you can start iterating on the more complex systems like graphics, sound, and extra levels. In the world of software development, especially today, three months is often enough to build something of any complexity. With modern tools, frameworks, and the power of AI, this timeline can be even shorter. For example, using AI tools to generate code snippets or automate certain aspects of the process can save time and help accelerate development.

The trick is to ensure that you're always working towards building and improving the core, rather than getting lost in flashy details or secondary features. By using task prioritization strategies that focus on the MVP and iterating in phases, you can significantly reduce development time and improve the overall quality of the product.

Trello for task management

Trello, especially the free version, is one of the most intuitive and user-friendly tools for task management. It's a fantastic choice for teams of any size, and I've used it myself in a variety of projects, including game development and hackathons. The simplicity of Trello lies in its Kanban board structure, which allows you to easily create, assign, and move tasks between columns like "**To Do**," "**In Progress**," and "**Done**." This makes it incredibly easy to visualize the workflow and track progress.

One of the best features of Trello's free version is that it doesn't overcomplicate things. You can quickly add tasks, attach files, set due dates, and create checklists without getting lost in excessive settings or complicated configurations. It's a great way to stay organized, especially when you're working with a small team or handling multiple projects at once.

Another advantage is its flexibility. Whether you're working on a game development project or a business software app, Trello allows you to adapt the board to your specific needs. For example, if you need to track bugs, features, or user stories, you can set up custom labels and columns accordingly.

While the free version has some limitations, like a cap on the number of Power-Ups (integrations) you can use, it still provides more than enough features to manage most small to medium-sized projects. For teams that don't need advanced reporting or automation features, Trello's free plan is ideal. It's easy to use, efficient, and will definitely keep you and your team on track.

Integrating task management with version control

Integrating task management with version control is essential for streamlining the development process, especially for larger projects or teams. By linking version control tools like GitHub or GitLab with task management platforms like Jira or Trello, you can automate various aspects of your workflow and ensure better synchronization between coding efforts and project progress.

In GitHub you can leverage GitHub Actions to automate repetitive tasks such as running tests, deployments, or updating task boards. When each task is associated with its own pull request (PR), it becomes easier to track progress. A PR should correspond to a specific task or feature, and by linking the PR to an issue in Jira or Trello, the task's status can be updated automatically as the work progresses.

Tools like GitHub's linked issues can connect commits or pull requests directly to tasks in Jira or Trello. As developers push changes, the corresponding issue will automatically update. This reduces the need for manual updates, keeping the task boards in sync with the codebase in real time.

Integrations also allow for task board automation. For example, when a PR is merged or closed in GitHub, workflows can automatically transition the associated Jira issues to another status or mark them as complete. This automation provides real-time updates without manual intervention and ensures both developers and project managers are always on the same page.

Tools such as *Jira's GitHub integration* allow the task management platform to automatically update an issue's status based on GitHub activity. This means when an issue is mentioned in a commit message, Jira updates the issue's progress accordingly. Integrating task management with version control ensures that development progress and task tracking stay aligned throughout the project's lifecycle.

By tying these systems together, you make the development workflow more efficient and less prone to errors. Tasks are automatically updated, tracked, and managed without the need for constant manual intervention, providing a seamless experience for the development team.

Agile task estimation

Task estimation in Agile, particularly the use of *story points*, can be a confusing concept, especially for developers who are used to thinking in terms of hours or days when estimating the time needed to complete a task. Story points, however, are part of a system designed to measure effort, complexity, and uncertainty rather than time. The idea is to estimate how difficult or complex a task will be compared to other tasks, rather than trying to predict exactly how long it will take.

The concept of story points is rooted in the idea that different team members might approach the same task differently based on their experience, skillset, and understanding of the project. Rather than having everyone guess the number of hours required, story points provide a common metric for the team to compare tasks and ensure that they're all on the same page.

To start, teams usually perform *planning poker*, a technique where every member of the team privately estimates the story points for a task. Once everyone has made their estimate, they reveal their guesses and discuss discrepancies. If there is a significant difference in estimates, the team discusses the reasons behind their numbers and arrives at a consensus. This process ensures that all team members understand the task's complexity and have the opportunity to voice any concerns.

Let's take an example to better understand how story points work. Suppose your team is tasked with implementing a simple form validation. One developer might think it will take a few hours, while another might estimate that it will take the entire day. By assigning story points, such as a 2-point task for the simple validation and a 5-point task for a complex form submission with validation and error handling, the team can focus on the relative difficulty of the task rather than getting bogged down in time-based estimates. The result? Everyone is on the same page about the scope of the task, even if they don't agree on exactly how many hours it will take.

The story point system is deliberately abstract. Rather than estimating exact time, it's designed to be a relative scale that can evolve over time. In a typical Agile workflow, story points are assigned to user stories based on the team's past experiences. If a developer works on a task and estimates it at 3 story points, and then realizes it was more complex than expected, the team may adjust its estimate for future tasks. This iterative process allows the team to refine its understanding of complexity over time.

The real beauty of story points is that they are not time-bound. While developers often fall into the trap of thinking about how long something will take, story points focus on the relative complexity of a task. This gives the team more flexibility and enables them to make decisions based on effort rather than strict time constraints. Over time, as a team works together, they gain a better understanding of their collective capabilities, which leads to more accurate estimations.

Velocity is another key concept tied to story points. Velocity refers to the number of story points a team can complete within a sprint. Teams track their velocity to understand how much work they can realistically handle in each sprint. By looking at the number of story points completed over previous sprints, the team can make better predictions about how much work they can take on in the future.

It's important to note that story points are not about tracking individual performance. Instead, they help teams understand how well they're performing collectively and identify areas for improvement. For instance, if a team consistently underestimates the complexity of tasks and their velocity decreases, this could signal that the team needs more time for certain tasks or that they need to adjust their approach. On the other hand, if they're completing tasks faster than expected, it might be an indication that they can handle more story points in the future.

While story points might seem abstract or even frustrating at first, the system is designed to help teams focus on relative complexity and collaborative understanding of tasks rather than worrying about time-based estimates. Over time, developers become more comfortable with estimating tasks in terms of story points, and the team builds better understanding and efficiency. It's essential for team members to embrace the estimation process and contribute their thoughts. Each person's unique experience and understanding of a task are valuable for arriving at a more accurate estimate.

For developers new to story points, it can take some time to adjust to the concept. But once you've worked through a few sprints and have had the chance to track your team's velocity, you'll see how story points provide a more reliable way to estimate work than traditional time-based estimation. Plus, the use of story points helps avoid the stress of rigidly trying to predict exactly how long a task will take. It encourages developers to think in terms of relative effort, complexity, and scope, making it easier to plan and adjust as the project progresses.

Chapter 11

Leveraging AI in Code Bookkeeping

AI tools for code analysis

AI tools for code analysis have revolutionized the way developers write and maintain code. The power of AI lies in its ability to instantly evaluate code for various issues, ranging from syntax errors to more complex problems like naming conventions, inefficient patterns, or code that doesn't align with industry best practices. Take my experience with *Rider IDE*, for example. While working on a project, I made some careless mistakes in naming conventions, and *Rider's AI-powered suggestions* immediately pointed them out. The recommendations not only helped improve the readability of the code but also ensured it adhered to proper standards, something that could be overlooked during long coding sessions.

Such tools are beneficial because they allow you to focus on the more creative and critical aspects of coding, while AI handles the repetitive and mundane tasks. These tools analyze the codebase at a pace much faster than any human can, and they provide instant feedback to help optimize the development process. This is what I refer to when I talk about *"10x development"*—where a developer can achieve much greater productivity by utilizing AI tools that support smarter coding practices.

So, don't just think of AI as a novelty or something that makes suggestions; it can be a real asset that helps elevate the quality of your code and improve overall efficiency.

Automated code reviews

Automated code reviews are a game-changer when it comes to maintaining the quality and consistency of a codebase. One of the most frustrating issues in manual code reviews is the bias or inconsistency in how reviewers approach large and small pull requests. A large pull request often gets a quick "accept" because reviewers are overwhelmed by the volume of code, while a small pull request might be nitpicked for even the smallest issues. This inconsistency can cause discrepancies in code quality across the project.

That's where automated code review tools come in. For instance, tools like *CodeFactor* on GitHub automatically assess the complexity of your code and provide instant feedback on potential issues. They can flag things like code duplication, overly complex methods, and potential performance bottlenecks, offering a uniform approach to code quality.

Moreover, with the rise of large language models (LLMs) like *OpenAI's Codex*, automated code review is taking another step forward. These tools can even generate suggestions on improving code structure, refactoring, and offering best practice recommendations, all based on a deeper understanding of the code. It's no longer just about catching syntax errors; it's about offering high-level insights into how to make your code more efficient and readable.

By integrating automated code reviews into your development process, you not only save time but also ensure that every pull request, regardless of size, is held to the same standard, leading to better, more maintainable code.

Predictive analytics for code issues

Predictive analytics tools for code issues are indeed a reality, and they are transforming how developers anticipate and address potential defects in software. These tools utilize machine learning algorithms to analyze historical code data, identify patterns, and predict areas of the codebase that are likely to contain defects. By leveraging such tools, development teams can proactively focus their testing and code review efforts on high-risk areas, thereby enhancing software quality and reducing the likelihood of post-release defects.

One notable example is *DeepCode*, an AI-powered tool designed to scan millions of lines of code to identify security flaws and other defects. It provides developers with actionable insights to fix issues before they become critical problems. (An AI Tool to Fix Those Pesky Software Defects, Draper)

Another example is *Defects AI*, a machine learning service that predicts issue types in GitHub repositories. By analyzing historical issue data, it can forecast potential defects, allowing teams to address them proactively. (Sascha Heyer, Medium)

Bugsplorer is a deep-learning technique that captures code contexts using hierarchical transformers to predict line-level defects. This approach enables teams to prioritize software quality assurance efforts on the most vulnerable areas of the codebase. (Parvez

Mahbub and Mohammad Masudur Rahman, Predicting Line-Level Defects by Capturing Code Contexts with Hierarchical Transformers)

These tools exemplify the integration of predictive analytics in software development, offering developers the capability to foresee and mitigate potential issues before they manifest, thereby streamlining the development process and enhancing code quality.

AI-driven testing

AI-driven testing has emerged as a revolutionary approach to software testing. The concept revolves around leveraging artificial intelligence to automate the generation of test cases based on existing code or specifications. AI tools can analyze code, understand its structure, and automatically generate test scenarios that cover edge cases, performance benchmarks, and error-prone areas. This helps reduce the burden on manual testers and ensures broader coverage with less effort.

One way AI can aid in testing is by automatically generating unit tests based on the functionality of a method or function. For example, tools like Diffblue utilize machine learning to generate unit tests in Java, understanding the logic in the code and crafting test cases that check various conditions.

Another use of AI-driven testing is in the creation of integration tests. AI can analyze dependencies and workflows between different components, automatically generating test scenarios that ensure all parts of the application interact correctly.

While AI-driven testing is impressive, it is not foolproof. Sometimes, AI tools might struggle to cover all the complex scenarios or context-specific conditions that a human tester might catch. It's important to use AI testing tools in conjunction with traditional manual testing methods to ensure comprehensive test coverage.

The future of AI-driven testing is promising, with more advanced algorithms and models being developed. These tools will likely become an indispensable part of the software development lifecycle, improving efficiency, accuracy, and speed of testing.

Future trends in AI and software development

As discussed in earlier sections about AI tools for code analysis and automated reviews, it's clear that AI is already reshaping how developers interact with their codebases. However, the impact of AI on software development goes far beyond these tools—it's fundamentally transforming the role of developers themselves.

AI systems are capable of generating code, suggesting improvements, and even predicting potential errors. Tools like GitHub Copilot, Rider's intelligent suggestions, and other language models have shown how AI can automate repetitive tasks, provide context-sensitive advice, and accelerate prototyping. These developments mark a shift where developers increasingly become managers of AI-driven workflows.

From Developer to AI Manager

This evolution changes what it means to be a developer. Instead of manually coding every aspect of a program, developers will define high-level objectives and oversee the AI's implementation. This managerial role requires a deep understanding of software architecture, problem definition, and AI behavior. As we've seen with code review tools, having a systematic approach is critical, and the same logic will extend to managing AI outputs.

In near future, AI may handle routine coding tasks while the developer focuses on framing complex problems, ensuring compliance with coding standards, and resolving edge cases. This shift in responsibilities emphasizes the need for explainable AI systems—tools that allow developers to monitor and understand the AI's decision-making process. Without transparency, the risk of errors or unintended behaviors increases, which could undermine trust in these systems.

Challenges Ahead

While AI offers enormous potential, it's not without its challenges. As we discussed in the section on predictive analytics, anticipating issues before they arise is essential. However, scaling this capability to the level of fully autonomous AI developers presents additional hurdles:

- **Job Shifts:** Traditional coding roles may decline as the focus moves to overseeing AI. This could lead to fewer entry-level opportunities for junior developers unless education systems adapt.
- **Quality Assurance:** The AI's ability to write code doesn't inherently guarantee quality. Developers must still validate the

outputs, emphasizing the importance of robust testing and review frameworks.

- **Ethical and Security Concerns:** AI-driven development must align with ethical standards and prioritize security. Ensuring fairness, avoiding biases, and safeguarding data integrity remain pressing concerns.

Future Tools for Developers

Incorporating lessons from our discussions on monitoring tools and analytics, future developers will rely on platforms that provide real-time feedback about what AI systems are doing. These platforms might include:

- **Transparent Dashboards:** Showing how AI makes decisions, what logic it employs, and where potential issues might arise.
- **Collaborative Workspaces:** Allowing developers to guide AI through iterative problem-solving processes.
- **Explainable AI Interfaces:** Making it easier to understand the AI's reasoning and ensuring its outputs align with the project's goals.

A New Era for Software Development

As AI continues to advance, the role of developers will increasingly focus on strategy and oversight. This aligns with earlier discussions on task management and prioritization, where planning and high-level decision-making are essential. AI will amplify the capacity of individual developers, enabling them to manage larger, more complex projects effectively

The future of software development is not just about writing code—it's about guiding intelligent systems to create better solutions.

Developers who adapt to this new paradigm will find themselves at the forefront of a revolutionary era, where creativity and leadership are as important as technical expertise. This shift, while challenging, holds incredible promise for those ready to embrace it.

Chapter 12

Writing Sustainable and Energy-Efficient Code

Green coding practices

Green coding, also known as *sustainable programming*, is a development approach that aims to minimize the environmental impact of software by optimizing energy consumption and resource utilization. In an era where data centers account for approximately 1% of global electricity consumption, inefficient software adds significantly to this burden. By adopting green coding practices, developers can contribute to a more sustainable future while creating more efficient and performant applications.

This concept builds on ideas discussed in earlier chapters, such as performance optimization and profiling, by adding a specific focus on energy usage. Green coding involves reducing unnecessary computational overhead, such as excessive CPU cycles or redundant memory operations. For example, a poorly optimized loop with unnecessary iterations can increase both processing time and energy consumption. Similarly, inefficient database queries or bloated file handling operations can lead to significant resource wastage.

The motivation behind green coding extends beyond environmental responsibility. Sustainable practices often result in faster and more scalable software, reducing infrastructure costs for organizations. Developers can leverage profiling tools to measure the energy consumption of their code and identify areas for improvement. This aligns closely with the principles of performance monitoring and debugging tools, which were detailed earlier in the book.

For those interested in exploring this field further, organizations like the Green Software Foundation offer valuable resources and insights. Academic research in energy-efficient computing, as well as practical guidance from communities such as IEEE and ACM, provides a deeper understanding of sustainable practices.

Green coding is not just about writing code that works but about writing code that works responsibly. By prioritizing energy efficiency and resource conservation, developers can ensure that technological progress aligns with the need for environmental sustainability.

Energy-efficient algorithms

Energy-efficient algorithms play a critical role in reducing the computational cost of solving problems while conserving resources. These optimizations are especially vital today, where large-scale applications such as machine learning models and real-time systems demand immense computational power.

The Need for Optimization

To understand the impact of algorithmic optimization, consider matrix multiplication, a fundamental operation in many domains, including graphics processing, machine learning, and scientific simulations. Algorithms that minimize redundant computations or utilize advanced techniques can significantly improve energy efficiency.

For instance, comparing traditional and optimized methods for multiplying matrices reveals a staggering difference in performance. In an experiment with two matrices of size 200, the traditional approach took approximately 4.93 seconds, while an optimized method using NumPy's built-in function completed the same task in just 0.00457 seconds. This represents a speedup of over 1,080 times! This level of efficiency is achieved by leveraging vectorization, caching strategies, and parallel computing within the optimized implementation.

Broader Implications

Such optimizations are not just about speed—they're about enabling possibilities. The energy saved by reducing computational overhead can be redirected towards other operations, enabling developers to scale applications sustainably. Moreover, these optimizations pave the way for new innovations. Imagine if machine learning models like large language models (LLMs) had to perform every operation without such efficient algorithms. Their feasibility would be greatly reduced, and their costs would skyrocket.

Optimization Begets Innovation

When existing solutions are optimized, they often inspire the development of entirely new algorithms. For example, Strassen's algorithm for matrix multiplication introduced sub-cubic time complexity for this operation, influencing advancements in computational complexity theory. Similarly, optimization in core operations leads to breakthroughs in applications like neural network training, real-time simulations, and large-scale data processing.

A Future Powered by Efficiency

We as developers, need to adopt and innovate around energy-efficient algorithms, both for sustainability and scalability. With tools like NumPy and similar libraries, adopting such practices has become more accessible than ever. By focusing on faster, more efficient solutions, we not only improve individual projects but also contribute to a broader effort to make computing greener and more sustainable.

Incorporating these optimizations into everyday coding practices ensures that our systems remain responsive and resource-friendly, enabling us to push the boundaries of innovation without overburdening the environment.

Measuring carbon footprint

When discussing the carbon footprint of code, it's important to understand that the environmental impact of software development goes beyond just the power consumption of the hardware it runs on. In fact, the energy consumed by a program during its execution can be directly linked to its efficiency. The more complex and resource-intensive the code, the greater the carbon footprint it generates. This is where concepts such as the time complexity of algorithms and the overall efficiency of code become pivotal.

One way to measure the carbon footprint of code is to assess its computational complexity and the resources it consumes. Time complexity, often expressed in Big O notation, is one such indicator. The higher the time complexity of an algorithm, the more processing power it requires, and consequently, the more energy it consumes. For instance, an O(n^2) algorithm, which grows quadratically with input size, will consume more resources than an O(n) algorithm, which grows linearly. This means that, when possible, reducing the time complexity of your algorithms isn't just about improving performance—it can also have a positive environmental impact by lowering the energy required to execute the program.

Another key factor is the execution time of the code. The longer a program runs, the more energy it consumes. If your application is performing tasks that require long-running processes, optimizing these operations to complete in less time can have a direct reduction in carbon emissions. The formula for energy consumption can be simplified to something like:

$$E = P \times t$$

Where E is energy, P is power consumption, and t is the time the process runs. In coding terms, reducing the time t through more efficient code can directly reduce the energy required for the task. A more efficient algorithm that takes less time to execute not only saves time for the user but also reduces the amount of power consumed by the hardware running the code.

One practical way to begin measuring the carbon footprint of your code is to focus on profiling tools that can give you an understanding of how much CPU and memory your application uses over time. These tools can provide insight into how your code's execution translates into energy consumption. For example, some cloud platforms provide carbon emissions calculators that allow you to assess the environmental impact of running specific code on their infrastructure. Similarly, there are tools that calculate the energy consumed per line of code or per function call.

Writing sustainable code involves more than just focusing on performance metrics. It's about considering how your choices in algorithmic design and execution impact the energy consumption of the systems that run your software. As software engineers, we must approach coding not only from the perspective of functionality and user experience but also with an awareness of the broader environmental impact. By optimizing code for both efficiency and sustainability, we can contribute to reducing the carbon footprint of software and building a more sustainable tech industry.

Optimizing resource usage

Optimizing resource usage is an essential aspect of software development that directly impacts the performance and sustainability of an application. Every application, whether small or large, utilizes system resources like CPU, memory, and network bandwidth. The key to effective resource usage is balancing performance with efficiency—ensuring that the application works well without unnecessarily consuming too much of these finite resources. Poorly optimized code can lead to slower execution, excessive energy consumption, and a degraded user experience. For example, memory leaks or excessive CPU usage can result in sluggish performance, and in some cases, even cause a system to crash.

Optimization should always be considered when there's clear evidence that a particular resource—whether it's time, memory, or CPU cycles—is being overused. However, it's important not to optimize prematurely. Focus on building a functional application first, and then use profiling tools to identify resource bottlenecks. These tools allow you to measure exactly where the inefficiencies lie and help pinpoint areas for improvement. Over-optimization before understanding the problem can complicate your code unnecessarily. The key is to make improvements that lead to noticeable and measurable improvements in performance, rather than optimizing every line of code without justification.

Efficient algorithms and data structures play a vital role in resource optimization. Selecting the right algorithm can drastically reduce both the time and space complexity of an application. For example, replacing a linear search ($O(n)$) with a binary search ($O(\log n)$) can lead to significant reductions in execution time when working with large datasets. Similarly, using a hash table for fast lookups rather than an array can decrease memory usage and improve the speed of access. Another essential optimization is memory management. If your program uses memory inefficiently—such as by holding on to large data structures for too long or neglecting to free memory when it's no longer needed—it can lead to high memory consumption and sluggish performance. This can be mitigated by ensuring resources are properly managed, and using data structures that are efficient in both time and space.

I/O operations often pose another significant source of inefficiency. For example, when an application repeatedly makes database queries or handles large file operations, it can quickly become a bottleneck. Optimizing I/O can involve reducing the number of database calls, utilizing batch processing, or even switching to asynchronous methods where applicable. These improvements can lead to faster execution and better use of system resources.

Optimizing resource usage, when done thoughtfully and at the right time, not only improves the performance of an application but also ensures that the software is scalable and energy-efficient. By being mindful of how the application interacts with system resources, developers can create more sustainable, high-performing software that works well across various environments and minimizes its environmental impact.

Sustainable software development principles

Sustainable software development principles focus on creating software that is not only effective but also mindful of long-term impact—on both the environment and the developers working on it. A key principle in sustainable software development is writing code that is clean, maintainable, and efficient. This ensures that the software can evolve over time without creating technical debt or overwhelming the development team. It's about striking a balance between short-term functionality and long-term sustainability, ensuring that updates, bug fixes, and future features can be added without compromising performance or causing excessive resource consumption.

A significant aspect of sustainability is optimizing code for efficiency, which reduces both energy consumption and the computational resources required for execution. Writing clear, concise, and modular code also contributes to sustainability by making it easier for other developers to maintain and extend the software. Sustainable software development is not only about creating applications that work well today but also about creating solutions that are future-proof and adaptable.

For readers looking to dive deeper into sustainable development practices, one excellent resource is the book "**The Sustainable Software Development**" by **Kevin Tate**. This book goes beyond just technical practices and provides insights on creating software that remains reliable and environmentally friendly over time. Tate emphasizes not only the environmental impact of code but also the importance of fostering a culture of sustainability within development teams. It's a practical and thoughtful read for anyone interested in applying sustainable principles to their development work.

Chapter 13

Secure Coding Practices in Code Bookkeeping

Secure coding standards

Secure coding is the practice of writing software in a way that safeguards it from security vulnerabilities and attacks. Unlike regular coding, which primarily focuses on functionality, performance, and maintainability, secure coding emphasizes identifying potential security flaws early in the development process and mitigating them before they can be exploited. This involves not just following best practices for clean, efficient code, but also considering the security implications of every line of code written. Secure coding aims to create applications that are resilient against various forms of malicious attacks, such as data breaches, denial of service, and unauthorized access.

The difference between regular coding and secure coding lies in the mindset of the developer. While regular coding focuses on delivering a working product as quickly as possible, secure coding requires developers to think ahead and anticipate potential threats. For example, where regular coding might focus on making a feature functional without considering input validation, secure coding emphasizes validating every piece of data that enters the system to prevent exploits like SQL injection or buffer overflow attacks. By integrating security measures throughout the development lifecycle, developers reduce the likelihood of introducing vulnerabilities into the codebase.

An excellent example of secure coding standards in action is the approach taken by NASA, one of the most security-conscious organizations. NASA's software engineering standards emphasize both secure coding and rigorous testing practices. The NASA Software Engineering Handbook outlines specific guidelines for secure coding, such as the avoidance of using insecure functions (like gets() in C), proper input validation, and using encryption for sensitive data. These standards also include ensuring that all code is thoroughly reviewed and tested for security vulnerabilities before being deployed. By adhering to strict coding standards, NASA ensures that its software is not only functional but also secure, given the critical nature of its missions where any vulnerability could have severe consequences.

Secure coding standards also encourage the use of proven libraries and tools that have been vetted for security and are regularly updated to address emerging threats. This helps developers avoid reinventing the wheel and reduces the risk of introducing new vulnerabilities by using insecure or outdated components. By integrating secure coding practices and standards, developers can build software that is robust, resilient, and prepared to withstand the ever-evolving landscape of cybersecurity threats.

Common vulnerabilities (SQL injection)

Being aware of common vulnerabilities is important in ensuring the security of the application. Vulnerabilities are weaknesses in the code that can be exploited by attackers to compromise the system. One of the most notorious vulnerabilities in software development is SQL injection, which occurs when an application allows attackers to manipulate a database query by injecting malicious SQL code. This can lead to unauthorized access, data leakage, or even complete system compromise. SQL injection exploits arise when user input is incorrectly handled and directly inserted into SQL queries, making it possible for attackers to manipulate the query and gain control over the database.

SQL injection is just one example of the many vulnerabilities developers need to be mindful of. Other common vulnerabilities include cross-site scripting (XSS), cross-site request forgery (CSRF), buffer overflows, and improper access controls. Each of these vulnerabilities presents unique security risks, but they share a common theme: the importance of validating and sanitizing user inputs. To prevent these issues, developers must take proactive steps to protect their code during development, rather than relying solely on testing or security scans after the code is completed.

The process of identifying and addressing vulnerabilities should start early—ideally during the coding phase—rather than waiting until the end. Incorporating secure coding practices, such as input validation and proper error handling, can go a long way toward preventing vulnerabilities from being introduced in the first place. This is where vulnerability assessment practices like VAPT (Vulnerability Assessment and Penetration Testing) come in. VAPT is a combination of automated scanning and manual testing designed to identify vulnerabilities in the code and network. By conducting VAPT, developers can catch potential issues before the software goes live, reducing the risk of exploitation.

A valuable resource for understanding and addressing vulnerabilities in code is the **OWASP Top Ten**. This well-known list from the **Open Web Application Security Project (OWASP)** highlights the most critical security risks for web applications, including SQL injection, broken authentication, and sensitive data exposure. The OWASP guidelines provide developers with clear, actionable advice on how to mitigate these risks, making it an invaluable tool for anyone focused on secure coding practices.

Vulnerabilities, such as SQL injection, should be actively sought and addressed during the development process. This proactive approach helps ensure that the application is secure and that vulnerabilities are not overlooked until it's too late. By adopting practices like input validation, using prepared statements for database queries, and leveraging tools like VAPT and OWASP resources, developers can significantly reduce the chances of their applications falling victim to common security threats.

Tools for security

When it comes to securing code, developers have access to a range of free tools that can help identify vulnerabilities, enforce security standards, and improve overall code quality. These tools allow you to assess your codebase for weaknesses, ensuring that security flaws like SQL injection, cross-site scripting (XSS), or buffer overflow vulnerabilities are caught early in the development process. This proactive approach to security is essential for building secure software, as highlighted in the earlier discussion about secure coding standards and common vulnerabilities.

One such tool is *OWASP ZAP* (Zed Attack Proxy), which is an open-source security tool designed specifically for finding vulnerabilities in web applications. While ZAP is typically used for penetration testing and identifying security flaws in a running web application, its static analysis features can be useful for scanning your code for common vulnerabilities such as SQL injection or XSS. As noted in the section on vulnerabilities, being proactive during the coding phase and identifying potential weaknesses before they reach production is key—and tools like OWASP ZAP help facilitate this.

Another useful tool is *SonarQube*, which offers static code analysis for detecting security flaws and code quality issues. SonarQube can be integrated into your build pipeline and automatically analyze your code for vulnerabilities such as hardcoded credentials, improper access controls, and other security risks. It provides a comprehensive overview of the security health of your codebase and highlights areas that need attention. It can be particularly helpful when used in conjunction with secure coding standards to maintain a secure, efficient codebase.

For developers working with JavaScript, *ESLint* can be an invaluable tool for ensuring that security best practices are being followed. *ESLint* is a linting tool that checks your code for potential errors and enforces coding standards. By integrating security-focused plugins, *ESLint* can also help identify patterns of insecure coding practices, such as unsanitized user inputs that could lead to SQL injection or XSS. Just as we discussed in the section on SQL injection, input validation is key to preventing many vulnerabilities, and tools like *ESLint* can help you catch common mistakes early.

Checkmarx is another tool worth mentioning, offering both free and paid options for static application security testing (SAST). The free version can scan your codebase for a wide range of vulnerabilities, helping developers identify and address security weaknesses early in the development cycle. It supports various programming languages and integrates with most CI/CD pipelines, allowing you to continuously monitor your code for security risks.

Snyk offers a free version that scans open-source dependencies for known vulnerabilities. Since many applications rely on external libraries, ensuring that these dependencies don't introduce security risks is vital. By using *Snyk*, developers can stay ahead of vulnerabilities that may be present in third-party packages, reducing the chances of introducing an external vulnerability into their own code.

For developers looking to learn more about securing their code, OWASP remains a crucial resource. As mentioned in previous sections, the OWASP Top Ten is a valuable guide that outlines the most common vulnerabilities and provides recommendations for addressing them. OWASP also offers various other tools and resources that can be useful for improving code security, such as the OWASP Dependency-Check for identifying vulnerable components in third-party libraries.

By integrating these free tools into the development workflow, developers can better manage security from the outset. They align well with the principles of secure coding discussed earlier, helping to build software that is both functional and resilient against common vulnerabilities.

Data protection best practices

Data protection is a critical aspect of secure software development, ensuring that sensitive information is kept safe from unauthorized access, theft, or loss. To protect data effectively, developers must implement best practices from the outset of the coding process. One of the key practices is encryption—ensuring that sensitive data, whether stored in databases or transmitted over networks, is always encrypted using strong algorithms. This prevents attackers from reading or tampering with the data even if they gain access to the system.

Another essential practice is to apply the principle of least privilege, ensuring that users and systems only have access to the data they absolutely need. This minimizes the potential damage caused by compromised accounts or systems. Additionally, securing data through proper input validation, as discussed earlier in the context of SQL injection, ensures that no malicious data can corrupt or exploit sensitive information.

For further guidance on data protection, the **OWASP Data Protection Cheat Sheet** provides a comprehensive set of recommendations for securing personal and sensitive data, such as guidelines for encryption, key management, and secure data storage. This resource is invaluable for developers looking to understand how to implement data protection throughout the software development lifecycle.

Chapter 14

Continuous Integration and Deployment: Automating Code Management

CI/CD pipeline setup

Setting up a CI/CD pipeline is a crucial step toward automating code management and streamlining the development lifecycle. However, it's important to understand when to integrate such a system into your project. As discussed earlier in Chapter 5, when focusing on continuous integration for testing, it's clear that CI/CD can be a game-changer once the application is ready for consistent deployment cycles. But is it something you should implement at the very beginning of your project?

In my experience, introducing a CI/CD pipeline too early, particularly during the prototype phase, can often slow down progress rather than accelerate it. As we explored in previous chapters, during the early stages of development, rapid prototyping and iterative changes are the focus. Setting up and maintaining a full CI/CD pipeline at this stage can be counterproductive. It diverts attention from building the core functionality of the product and can create additional overhead. For example, configuring automated tests, deployment scripts, and integration points can be time-consuming, and when the codebase is still evolving rapidly, it may be difficult to keep these pipelines up-to-date.

> *"It's only once you're past the prototype phase, when your application is stable enough to start moving towards regular updates and deployment, that implementing a CI/CD pipeline becomes truly beneficial."*

At this point, automating the build, test, and deployment process allows your team to focus more on developing features rather than managing repetitive tasks. In a mature development environment, where the project has clear milestones and a structured plan for delivery, a CI/CD pipeline ensures smoother, faster, and more reliable deployments, and it allows you to detect issues earlier, particularly with automated testing and version control integration, as discussed earlier in the chapter.

Once the project is near the stage where regular deployment is expected, setting up the pipeline becomes a natural next step. Not only does it help ensure that each commit is validated through automated testing, but it also ensures that the deployment process is as efficient and error-free as possible. By then, the code is more refined, and the benefits of CI/CD—such as reduced deployment time, fewer manual errors, and faster delivery cycles—become clear. So, rather than rushing into CI/CD setup from day one, it's better to wait until the project is stable enough to support it effectively, ensuring that the pipeline enhances your workflow without creating unnecessary complexity.

Deployment strategies (blue-green deployment)

Blue-green deployment is a deployment strategy designed to minimize downtime and reduce the risk of introducing errors into a live production environment. The core idea behind blue-green deployment is to have two identical production environments, referred to as the "blue" environment and the "green" environment. At any given time, one environment is live (serving production traffic), while the other is idle or used for testing.

The process begins by deploying the new version of the application to the idle environment, which is typically the green environment. This allows you to test the new version in an environment identical to production, ensuring that everything works as expected without disrupting the active environment (the blue environment). Once testing is complete and you're confident that the new version is stable, you switch the traffic from the blue environment to the green environment. This switch can be done seamlessly, often with just a few configuration changes or DNS updates, which leads to minimal downtime.

Imagine you're running an e-commerce application with high traffic. You want to deploy a new version of your website, but you can't afford any downtime. Using the blue-green deployment strategy, you would deploy the new version of the website to the green environment. After thoroughly testing the green environment to ensure it behaves as expected, you switch all user traffic from the current blue environment to the newly updated green environment. If any issues arise in the green environment after the switch, you can quickly revert to the blue environment, which is still running the old version of the application. This rollback is nearly instantaneous, which minimizes disruption for your users.

One significant benefit of blue-green deployment is the ability to perform a smooth, controlled release with zero downtime. If issues are detected post-deployment, you can quickly roll back to the previous stable environment without impacting the user experience. Additionally, because both environments are identical, you can test performance and load handling in the green environment, ensuring that the new version is capable of handling production traffic before it goes live.

This strategy also supports continuous integration and deployment pipelines, as it allows you to deploy, test, and roll back changes quickly, enabling rapid iteration and faster releases. By using blue-green deployment, you can ensure your users always experience a stable version of the application, reducing the risks associated with introducing new code into production.

Incorporating blue-green deployment into your workflow not only improves your release process but also helps maintain a high level of service reliability. It aligns well with the principles of continuous integration and deployment, as we discussed earlier, and provides an effective way to manage risk during application updates.

Monitoring CI/CD processes

Monitoring CI/CD processes is essential for ensuring that your pipeline is running smoothly and efficiently. It allows you to track the health of your builds, deployments, and overall delivery pipeline in real time. Effective monitoring helps catch issues early, whether it's a failing test, a build that's taking too long, or a deployment that's stuck. Without proper monitoring, you risk missing critical performance issues or security vulnerabilities that could affect the reliability and speed of your software delivery.

A great solution for this is *GitLab CI/CD*, which offers an intuitive and powerful dashboard to monitor your entire CI/CD pipeline. GitLab's dashboard provides real-time insights into each stage of the pipeline, from code commits to build and deployment. It allows you to visualize the success rate of builds, the time it takes for deployments, and the overall health of the pipeline, all in one place. This kind of dashboard as a service (SaaS) solution helps streamline the monitoring process by giving developers an easy way to track issues and make informed decisions about the next steps.

Similarly, *CircleCI* offers a robust monitoring interface that tracks and visualizes your builds, test results, and deployments. The *CircleCI* dashboard is designed to be user-friendly and provides detailed logs and metrics that allow you to identify bottlenecks, failure points, and overall trends in your CI/CD processes. By integrating such tools into your workflow, you ensure that your CI/CD pipeline remains transparent and manageable, keeping the entire development process optimized and error-free.

Integrating CI/CD with version control

CI/CD and Git serve distinct but complementary roles in modern development workflows. Git, primarily a version control tool, helps developers manage code, track changes, and collaborate. It's an essential part of any project, enabling the team to keep track of the history and evolution of their codebase. However, just using Git doesn't imply that you're practicing CI/CD.

CI/CD, on the other hand, is an automation framework that goes beyond version control. It focuses on automating the process of building, testing, and deploying code. While Git manages versions and tracks changes, CI/CD tools like *GitHub Actions, Vercel, and Netlify* automate the workflow, such as running tests, building the application, and pushing it live to production whenever certain rules are met, like code being merged into a main branch. These tools act on Git repositories and can trigger actions automatically based on code changes.

If you're implementing CI/CD, it's almost guaranteed you're using Git for version control as well. However, using Git by itself doesn't set up an automated process for testing or deployment. CI/CD tools integrate tightly with Git, but the key difference is automation and ensuring smooth, error-free deployments, something Git alone can't do.

Chapter 15

Essential Tools and Resources for Code Bookkeeping

Tools for version control

Version control is a foundational element in any software development process. It allows developers to track changes in their codebase, collaborate efficiently with team members, and maintain a reliable history of their project. Most developers are familiar with Git, as it has become the industry standard for version control, largely due to its distributed nature and powerful branching and merging capabilities. Git enables teams to work independently on their code, while also ensuring that all changes are tracked, and versions can be rolled back if necessary.

However, *Git* is not the only version control tool available. While we've covered Git extensively in earlier chapters, it's important to acknowledge other tools that offer different approaches to version control. For example, *Mercurial* is another distributed version control system that shares many similarities with Git, such as its ability to track changes and manage multiple branches. Though Git has gained more widespread adoption, Mercurial still has a strong user base, particularly in certain industries or organizations that prioritize its simplicity and ease of use.

As we discussed in earlier chapters, choosing the right version control system depends on your project's needs. The tools we use for version control provide the backbone for code management, but the way we set them up and integrate them with our workflows can vary depending on the size and structure of the team, as well as the nature of the project.

While Git and Mercurial may be the most commonly known, there are also centralized systems like *Subversion* (SVN), which work differently from the distributed systems we've mentioned. In SVN, all developers share a central repository, which can make it easier to manage, but also introduces some limitations around branching and offline work. These tools, whether distributed or centralized, serve as the foundation for collaborating on code, and choosing the right one is an essential first step in implementing effective version control.

In future case studies, we'll take a closer look at how different version control systems, such as Mercurial, fit into real-world scenarios and how they compare with Git in practical applications. For now, though, it's essential to understand that version control is not just about Git—it's about the principles of managing code changes and the tools that help us achieve this goal, each offering unique benefits based on the requirements of your project and team.

Code analysis

Code analysis is an essential practice for maintaining high-quality, secure, and efficient software. By analyzing code, developers can identify potential issues, improve performance, and ensure that best practices are being followed. While code analysis can take many forms, from static to dynamic analysis, the key is to use tools that automate the process and help catch errors early in the development cycle.

One of the most common forms of code analysis is static analysis, where the code is examined without being executed. Static analysis tools can examine your codebase for a wide range of issues, such as coding standard violations, security vulnerabilities, and performance bottlenecks. Tools like *SonarQube* and *Codacy* are widely used in the industry for static code analysis. These tools can be integrated into your CI/CD pipeline to continuously monitor the health of your codebase. As we've seen in earlier chapters, ensuring that the code adheres to best practices is not just about aesthetics or style, but about making it maintainable, secure, and scalable.

In contrast, dynamic analysis looks at the behavior of the code while it's running. This type of analysis often involves testing the application under various conditions to identify runtime errors, memory leaks, and performance issues. Tools like *Valgrind* and Dynatrace help developers understand how their application behaves in real-time, providing insights that static analysis can't.

Linters are tools that automatically scan your code for syntax and style issues as you write it. These tools help ensure that your code is not only functional but also readable and consistent, reducing the risk of bugs and improving overall maintainability.

By incorporating code analysis tools into your workflow, whether static or dynamic, you can improve code quality, detect vulnerabilities, and ensure your software is optimized for both performance and security. It's a critical step, one that complements the principles of version control and secure coding, which we explored in previous chapters, providing a comprehensive approach to maintaining high standards throughout the development lifecycle.

Testing

Each programming language has its own set of frameworks designed to facilitate writing and running tests efficiently. These frameworks provide tools for unit testing, integration testing, and even more complex testing workflows. Let's look at some of the popular testing frameworks across various languages.

In Python, one of the most widely used testing frameworks is *pytest*. It is highly favored for its simplicity, ease of use, and powerful features like fixtures, parameterized testing, and excellent integration with CI/CD pipelines. Another popular framework in Python is *unittest*, which is part of the standard library and follows the *xUnit* model for test organization and execution.

For JavaScript, *Jest* is the go-to framework, especially for testing React applications. It is known for its speed and ability to mock functions easily, making it ideal for unit and integration tests. Other notable testing libraries in JavaScript include *Mocha* (a flexible framework with a wide range of plugins) and Jasmine, which provides a behavior-driven development (BDD) style for writing tests.

In the world of Java, the most commonly used testing framework is JUnit. *JUnit* provides an easy way to organize tests, assert conditions, and set up test environments. It integrates seamlessly into build systems like Maven and Gradle, making it ideal for Java projects. TestNG is another option, offering more advanced features like parallel test execution and test configuration.

For C#, *NUnit* and *xUnit* are two of the most prominent testing frameworks. Both follow the xUnit architecture, providing support for data-driven tests, assertions, and setup/teardown functionality. *MSTest*, Microsoft's own framework, is also commonly used, particularly in the context of Visual Studio development.

In C++, *Google Test* is one of the most popular frameworks. It supports a variety of test types and provides advanced features like assertions, mock objects, and exception testing. Another notable framework is Catch2, known for its simplicity and ease of use for unit testing in C++.

For Rust, *Cargo test* is the default testing framework, integrated directly into the language's package manager, Cargo. It provides support for unit testing, benchmarking, and integration testing. Rust's testing tools are designed to be minimalistic, following the language's philosophy of simplicity and performance.

Each of these frameworks, as we discussed in previous chapters, contributes to ensuring that your code is robust, maintainable, and reliable. They provide developers with powerful tools for automating tests, catching bugs early, and enhancing the quality of their software.

Monitoring

It's crucial to have the right tools to keep track of your code's performance, identify errors, and ensure that everything runs smoothly in production. Monitoring allows you to catch issues early, optimize performance, and make data-driven decisions for further development. For many developers, this involves using specialized packages or frameworks that provide detailed insights into how their applications are performing.

For those working with Python, I highly recommend checking out my package, *Trace Book*. Trace Book is designed for comprehensive code bookkeeping, allowing you to log critical information such as function calls, parameters, return values, and execution times. It also supports decorators for easy integration, making it simple to add monitoring functionality to your existing codebase. One of its standout features is its automatic error tracking and remote log transmission, ensuring that you're notified when things go wrong— without having to manually check logs. The package also provides customizable log levels and output configurations, allowing you to tailor the level of detail based on your needs.

Trace Book is a practical solution for developers who want a simple yet powerful way to keep track of their code's behavior. Whether you're monitoring a small project or a large application, Trace Book helps you maintain a comprehensive view of what's happening behind the scenes. You can integrate it seamlessly into your development process and use it to enhance your ability to troubleshoot and optimize your code.

While Trace Book is a Python-specific tool, other programming languages have their own monitoring solutions. For example, Prometheus and Grafana are widely used for monitoring and alerting in cloud-native applications, providing rich visualizations and a flexible alerting system. In JavaScript, tools like New Relic and Datadog offer comprehensive monitoring for web applications, tracking everything from server performance to user interactions.

By integrating effective monitoring into your development workflow, you can ensure that you have the necessary insights to keep your code running smoothly, whether you're troubleshooting errors, optimizing performance, or simply keeping track of how your application behaves in production.

Learning resources (books, online courses, industry blogs)

It is good to have access to the right resources. While this book covers a lot, it's important to note that there are countless other books, online courses, and blogs that delve deeper into topics like maintaining code, migration strategies, and efficient version control. As we discussed earlier, keeping your codebase organized, secure, and efficient requires ongoing learning, and these resources can help you take your skills to the next level.

One of the first books that come to mind is **Clean Code: A Handbook of Agile Software Craftsmanship** by **Robert C. Martin**. This classic offers invaluable advice on how to write clean, maintainable code that stands the test of time. It's a must-read for any developer who wants to avoid the pitfalls of messy, hard-to-maintain code. Building on that, **Code Complete** by **Steve McConnell** is another great read, diving deep into the practices and principles of software construction, which is essential when managing a growing codebase. These books provide timeless advice, much like what we explored in earlier chapters, emphasizing the importance of organizing your code in a way that keeps it maintainable and scalable.

One great resource is **Model-Driven Software Migration: A Methodology** by **Christian W. L. Hill**. This book lays out a methodology for software migration, which we touched upon when discussing the challenges of maintaining and evolving legacy code. Understanding how to modernize and migrate code safely is essential for anyone working with long-term projects. If you're more interested in web applications and front-end work, **Atomic Migration Strategy for Web Teams** by **Brad Frost** provides practical insights into how to apply atomic design principles to web application migrations, focusing on low-risk strategies.

There are numerous online courses that can enhance your knowledge. Platforms like **Udemy** and **Pluralsight** offer in-depth courses on version control, maintaining clean code, and agile practices. For example, you can find courses that teach best practices in version control systems like Git, which we explored in Chapter 2, and take a closer look at migration strategies used in modern applications.

Another excellent way to stay updated and informed is through industry blogs. Blogs like Martin Fowler's Refactoring, Joel on Software, and The Daily WTF provide ongoing discussions around code quality, refactoring, and real-world coding challenges. These blogs offer insight into how industry experts approach the ever-evolving world of software development. They not only provide technical tips but also address the broader principles of keeping codebase management both effective and sustainable.

These resources are just a few examples of the wealth of material available to help you refine your skills in code bookkeeping, maintenance, and migration. As we have seen throughout this book, keeping your codebase clean, efficient, and up to date is a continuous process that benefits from both knowledge and practice. Whether you prefer to read, watch, or interact, there's a resource to fit your learning style and further your journey in software development.

Chapter 16

Case Studies

Real-world case studies, (monorepo structure of google and facebook, other structures)

When we explore the real-world application of code structures, one of the most notable examples comes from Google and Facebook. Both companies use monorepo structures to manage their massive codebases, and the lessons learned from their implementations offer valuable insights into how large organizations can manage complex, interconnected systems efficiently.

A monorepo is a version control system setup where all of a company's code, including multiple projects, services, and libraries, is stored in a single repository. Google, for instance, manages over two billion lines of code within its monorepo, an impressive scale that showcases the potential of this approach. By housing everything in one place, Google ensures that teams work from the same codebase, creating consistency and reducing issues like dependency mismatches and version conflicts.

The advantages of a monorepo, as we saw earlier in the context of version control in Chapter 2, include simplified dependency management. Instead of managing separate repositories for various services, a monorepo allows for centralized control, making it easier to update shared libraries or components without risking synchronization issues across different parts of the organization. In Google's case, this means that when a change is made to a shared component, it's instantly reflected throughout the entire company, avoiding discrepancies and reducing the overhead of managing separate repositories.

The challenges of managing a monorepo are not insignificant. One of the most common issues, is the scalability of the version control and build systems themselves. Managing a monorepo of Google's scale requires custom-built tools designed to handle such vast codebases efficiently. For example, *Piper* is the version control system Google has developed to handle the complexities of merging changes, managing builds, and running tests. Similarly, *Bazel*, Google's build tool, is optimized for large-scale development and is capable of performing incremental builds, reducing the risk of long build times that could hinder development speed.

Facebook, on the other hand, began with a polyrepo setup and eventually transitioned to a monorepo for similar reasons. Their decision was driven by the need for greater collaboration between teams, as well as the difficulty of maintaining separate repositories for services that were deeply interdependent. The React framework is a great example of this approach. Facebook's transition to a monorepo allowed them to make global updates to React across multiple projects quickly and seamlessly. By using a monorepo, Facebook ensured that their teams could avoid the headache of managing multiple versions of shared components while also enabling faster collaboration on updates.

Yet, as we saw earlier in Chapter 5, testing and continuous integration become even more critical in a monorepo setup. For companies like Google and Facebook, ensuring that new changes do not break existing functionality across multiple projects is paramount. That's where their custom CI tools come into play. For

Facebook, Buck is used to manage builds and tests, and it plays a key role in reducing the risk of long test cycles by ensuring that only the changed parts of the code are rebuilt.

Despite the benefits, not every company needs a monorepo. Smaller teams or those with less interdependent services might find a polyrepo structure more effective. A polyrepo allows for simpler, more isolated project management, where each service or project has its own repository, reducing complexity. However, the trade-off is that shared dependencies across services can become harder to manage, especially as your codebase grows.

For companies considering whether to move to a monorepo structure, it's important to weigh the trade-offs carefully. As we discussed in earlier chapters, scalability and team collaboration are key factors to consider. A monorepo can significantly enhance these areas, but it requires investment in specialized tools, robust testing frameworks, and careful planning to ensure that it doesn't become a burden rather than a benefit.

We'll take a deeper dive into how these repository structures play out in real-world applications. For now, it's essential to remember that whether you choose a monorepo or a polyrepo, the goal should always be to find the structure that best supports your team's workflow and the long-term maintainability of your codebase.

Lessons learned from experts

When looking at the way experts approach software development, there are countless lessons to be learned. Over the years, many developers and thought leaders in the field have shared invaluable insights that can help guide both new and experienced programmers toward better practices. These lessons go beyond just writing functional code; they touch on everything from maintaining clean codebases to adopting efficient workflows and preparing for long-term scalability.

One of the most enduring lessons comes from Robert C. Martin, also known as "Uncle Bob," whose work on Clean Code has had a profound influence on software engineering. One of his key messages is that code is not just written for machines—it's written for humans who will need to read, understand, and maintain it. According to Martin, the single most important factor for a sustainable codebase is readability. Clean, readable code minimizes the mental effort needed to understand it, which reduces the likelihood of bugs and makes it easier to introduce changes. This is something we've touched upon earlier in the book when discussing the importance of code organization and naming conventions.

Another important lesson from experts like Martin Fowler, known for his work on Refactoring, is the idea that you should never hesitate to improve your code—especially when it comes to refactoring. Fowler emphasizes that refactoring is not just about fixing bugs but about continuously improving the design of your software. By regularly revisiting and refactoring your code, you ensure that your software can adapt to new requirements without becoming unmanageable or convoluted. This concept ties directly into the discussion of sustainable and maintainable code we explored in Chapter 12, where we examined how to write code that can evolve over time without introducing technical debt.

From Kent Beck, the creator of Test-Driven Development (TDD), we learn that the process of writing tests before writing code can dramatically improve software quality. Beck argues that TDD forces developers to think about their code's behavior upfront, leading to better design and fewer bugs in the long run. While we've covered the importance of testing in earlier chapters, particularly in Chapter 5 on Test Cases, Beck's philosophy underscores the critical role testing plays in keeping codebase integrity intact. TDD isn't just about ensuring the code works; it also makes it easier to refactor, as you can be confident that the tests will catch any mistakes or regressions.

Experts also emphasize the importance of collaboration and communication within development teams. One such lesson comes from **Joel Spolsky**, the co-founder of Trello, who has been vocal about the necessity of good communication in software development. According to Spolsky, maintaining an open and collaborative environment leads to better decision-making, higher morale, and ultimately, more successful projects. This resonates with the agile methodologies we explored in Chapter 6, where we discussed the importance of iterative development and continuous feedback in delivering high-quality software.

Another key piece of advice from the experts revolves around code reviews. As we discussed earlier, code reviews are crucial for maintaining code quality and ensuring that best practices are being followed. Industry leaders like **Jeff Atwood**, co-founder of Stack Overflow, have highlighted how code reviews can act as learning opportunities for both junior and senior developers. By reviewing code, developers expose themselves to new perspectives, spot potential issues early, and ensure that the codebase remains consistent across teams.

Lastly, **Martin Odersky**, the creator of the Scala programming language, teaches us the importance of balancing simplicity with scalability. Odersky stresses that it's easy to over-engineer software by introducing unnecessary complexity in an effort to future-proof it. However, complexity often leads to more maintenance work and higher chances of failure. The key, as he advocates, is to build software that meets current needs and is flexible enough to adapt to future requirements without becoming overly complex. This is something we've alluded to throughout the book, particularly when discussing design patterns and SOLID principles.

These lessons from software development experts emphasize the importance of clean, readable, and maintainable code, as well as the value of testing, collaboration, and continuous improvement. They provide a solid foundation for building software that stands the test of time and adapts to changing requirements, which is what we've been exploring in this book. By embracing these lessons and applying them consistently, developers can avoid common pitfalls and create robust, scalable, and sustainable codebases.

Best practices in action

When entering the software development world, it's easy to feel overwhelmed by the myriad of practices and tools available. However, by understanding and adopting certain best practices from leading companies, even freshers can quickly make an impact in their work and contribute to the efficiency and quality of the codebase. These best practices are the cornerstone of sustainable development, offering both short-term and long-term benefits for personal growth and project success.

One of the most important best practices, emphasized by major companies like Google and Facebook, is the use of version control systems, particularly Git. In many organizations, Git is a non-negotiable tool, as it's crucial for tracking changes, enabling collaboration, and managing different versions of the codebase. For freshers, learning Git early on is essential. It's not just about committing code, but understanding workflows like branching and pull requests, which are fundamental in collaborative environments. For instance, Gitflow—a branching strategy that organizes feature development, bug fixes, and releases—ensures that multiple developers can work on the same project without stepping on each other's toes. Practicing this workflow can help a fresher seamlessly integrate into a development team and avoid conflicts or issues related to code integration.

Another key practice is code reviews. Companies like Microsoft and Netflix rely heavily on peer code reviews to maintain high-quality standards in their codebases. For freshers, this is not just an opportunity to learn from more experienced developers, but also a chance to develop a mindset for writing clean, understandable, and maintainable code. Code reviews should be seen as collaborative, constructive conversations, rather than a critical evaluation. Freshers can benefit from understanding that reviews are meant to improve code quality, catch bugs early, and ensure consistency across the codebase. A company that prioritizes peer reviews is one that values transparency and collective ownership of the code, and this practice will help newcomers improve their coding skills rapidly.

Furthermore, automated testing is another best practice widely adopted by companies like Facebook and Spotify. Freshers should focus on writing unit tests, integration tests, and end-to-end tests to ensure their code is bug-free and functional. These companies have integrated automated testing into their workflows, ensuring that code changes don't break existing functionality. Learning to write tests early on, particularly using tools like Jest (for JavaScript), pytest (for Python), or JUnit (for Java), is an invaluable skill. This practice not only prevents regression errors but also fosters a mindset of thinking about edge cases and robustness when developing software.

For freshers looking to improve their development practices, pair programming is a technique that many companies, including XP (Extreme Programming) teams, have found to be highly effective. Pair programming involves two developers working on the same task, with one writing the code while the other reviews and provides feedback in real-time. It fosters collaboration, improves code quality, and allows freshers to quickly absorb best practices from their peers. It's a great opportunity for learning, particularly for those starting in the field, as it accelerates the learning process and exposes new developers to different perspectives and solutions.

In addition, a focus on documentation is a practice often seen in top companies like Amazon and Dropbox. Freshers should be encouraged to document not only the code they write but also their thought processes, design decisions, and any tricky problems they encounter. Well-written documentation ensures that others can follow their work, even if they're not involved in the same project. It also aids in troubleshooting, making the codebase more understandable and maintainable in the long term. Learning to write clear, concise documentation is a key part of becoming a professional developer.

Companies like Google and GitHub are also known for embracing continuous integration and continuous deployment (CI/CD) practices. These practices help automate the process of integrating new code changes, running automated tests, and deploying the code to production. As a fresher, understanding the importance of CI/CD can help in building reliable software quickly. Familiarity with CI/CD tools like Jenkins, Travis CI, or GitHub Actions will allow you to contribute to faster development cycles and ensure that the code you write is always in a deployable state.

Finally, it's essential to understand and adopt the principle of code simplicity. Many companies, including Netflix, emphasize simplicity in their codebases to ensure scalability and maintainability. Freshers should avoid overengineering solutions and instead focus on writing straightforward, clear code that solves the problem at hand without unnecessary complexity. Simple code is easier to understand, debug, and extend, and it helps in the long-term health of the project. As discussed in earlier chapters, focusing on clean, readable, and well-organized code should be a constant goal throughout your development career.

By adopting these best practices—version control, code reviews, automated testing, pair programming, documentation, CI/CD, and code simplicity—freshers can set themselves up for success in the fast-paced, collaborative world of software development. These practices are not only the foundation of high-quality code but also the habits that will help you grow as a developer, contributing meaningfully to projects and continuously improving your craft.

Common pitfalls and avoidance

In software development, avoiding common pitfalls is just as important as following best practices. One of the most frequent mistakes developers make is failing to prioritize readability. Writing code that works is not enough; it should also be easy to read and understand, especially when collaborating with others. To avoid this, always follow consistent naming conventions and modularize your code to enhance clarity, as discussed earlier in the book.

Another common pitfall is neglecting testing. Relying solely on manual testing or skipping it entirely can lead to undetected bugs and issues down the road. As we've seen, automating tests as part of the CI/CD pipeline is essential for ensuring code quality and avoiding costly regressions.

Lastly, developers often fall into the trap of over-engineering. Adding unnecessary complexity in an effort to future-proof your code can make it harder to maintain and scale. Instead, focus on simplicity and clarity, solving the current problem without trying to account for every possible future scenario.

By being mindful of these pitfalls and actively working to avoid them, developers can create more efficient, maintainable, and scalable software.

Practical tips for implementation

When starting out in software development, it's easy to feel overwhelmed by the wealth of practices and tools available. As we've covered throughout the book, implementing everything at once is not only impractical but also unnecessary. For newbies, it's essential to start small and build a solid foundation before diving into more complex practices.

The first thing you should focus on is version control. Mastering Git is critical, as it enables you to track changes, collaborate with others, and manage your code effectively. Once you're comfortable with Git, the next step is to write automation scripts to help speed up repetitive tasks. This could be anything from automating builds to running unit tests. Starting with simple scripts will help you understand automation's role in development and increase your productivity.

As you become more confident, gradually introduce automated tests into your workflow. Begin with basic unit tests, and as your project grows, expand to integration and end-to-end tests. Automated testing ensures the stability of your codebase and reduces the risk of introducing bugs during development.

As your project matures and the codebase grows, you can start adopting more advanced practices like CI/CD, code reviews, and monitoring tools. However, it's crucial to approach these implementations gradually, integrating them as your project's needs evolve. This incremental approach will allow you to build a robust, maintainable, and scalable development process without feeling overwhelmed.

Chapter 17

Building a Culture of Code Bookkeeping

Key takeaways summary

As we conclude this journey into code bookkeeping, we've covered a range of topics that touch on the core principles of maintaining a clean, efficient, and scalable codebase. What we've learned is that good code management isn't just a set of isolated practices—it's a mindset and a culture that permeates every part of software development.

At the heart of code bookkeeping lies the idea that code should be organized, maintainable, and adaptable. We've explored how version control systems like Git are the backbone of managing code, allowing teams to track changes, collaborate efficiently, and avoid chaos. We discussed the importance of code structure and organization, including modular programming, proper folder structures, and the need for clear documentation, all of which contribute to a codebase that is easy to navigate and extend.

Throughout the book, we've emphasized the value of adhering to best practices—whether it's naming conventions, following SOLID principles, or continuously refactoring code to keep it clean. We've seen how automated testing ensures that the software we write is robust, while continuous integration and deployment make it easier to release stable versions of software faster and more reliably. These practices aren't just beneficial—they're essential for scaling and maintaining a healthy codebase.

We've also touched on security, sustainability, and monitoring—vital areas that ensure the software is not only functional but secure, efficient, and adaptable in a rapidly changing environment. As we explored in the case studies, companies like Google and Facebook show us the importance of structuring code in ways that are scalable, both in terms of infrastructure and human collaboration. AI-driven tools are on the horizon to help developers automate repetitive tasks, analyze code quality, and predict potential issues, making the future of software development both exciting and efficient.

The key takeaway from all these discussions is the importance of creating a culture of code bookkeeping within teams. It's about fostering a mindset where code is treated as a long-term asset, not just a short-term solution to a problem. As developers, we must embrace continuous learning and always strive to improve our practices. No one can implement everything at once, but gradually adopting these practices over time will set you on the path to writing code that is maintainable, secure, and scalable.

For those just starting out, focus on the fundamentals—master version control, get comfortable with writing tests, and embrace automation as you grow in your career. As your projects scale, begin to integrate more advanced practices, whether it's setting up a CI/CD pipeline, adopting Agile methodologies, or using AI tools to help manage your codebase.

The future of code management is bright. With continuous advancements in automation, artificial intelligence, and best practices for code management, the process of building software will only become more efficient, secure, and sustainable. By embracing the culture of code bookkeeping, you ensure that the software you create will stand the test of time.

Encouraging a code bookkeeping culture

What we've learned about code bookkeeping throughout this book isn't just theory or abstract advice—it's a fundamental truth that every developer, whether you're writing or reading code, will inevitably need to go through. Code bookkeeping, or the practice of organizing, managing, and maintaining code systematically, is not an optional task but a crucial part of any development process. It's what ensures that the codebase remains functional, scalable, and maintainable over time.

The truth is, as a developer, whether you're working on your own or as part of a team, you're bound to encounter situations where good code management practices will save you time, reduce errors, and increase productivity. Every project, regardless of its size, will eventually need version control, testing, documentation, and consistent structure. The habits we've discussed—such as using version control systems, adhering to naming conventions, and implementing automated tests—are not just best practices for high-level projects, they are the building blocks for even the smallest applications.

The key here is to start small and implement basic code bookkeeping principles in your current projects. If you're just beginning your journey, focus on simple things like organizing your codebase into logical modules, writing meaningful commit messages in Git, and adding basic tests to ensure functionality.

These may seem like small tasks now, but as your project grows, they will lay a solid foundation for future development and scaling.

Encourage yourself to adopt these practices early on in your career. By starting with small steps, you'll find that code bookkeeping becomes second nature, making it easier to manage and extend your projects as they evolve. Over time, the tools, techniques, and principles discussed here will help you become a more efficient, organized, and thoughtful developer. It's a habit that pays off, not only in the success of your projects but also in the ease with which you and your team can adapt, collaborate, and innovate.

So, as you continue to work on your projects, remember that code bookkeeping is not just something you do when the codebase becomes "too big" or "too complicated." It's something that should be integrated into your daily coding habits, no matter the size or scope of your project. By embracing this culture now, you set yourself up for a future where you are not only writing code but managing it in a way that ensures long-term success and sustainability.

Importance of continuous learning

In the ever-evolving world of programming, the importance of continuous learning cannot be overstated. As I've mentioned before, the rapid pace of technological advancements makes it crucial for developers to keep up with new tools, languages, and frameworks. A perfect example of this is the existence of a website called dayssincelastjavascriptframework.com, which humorously counts how long it's been since the last JavaScript framework was released. This shows just how quickly the landscape of development changes, and how you need to adapt yourself to what comes next.

Right now, as we speak, we are in the AI era, and the power of artificial intelligence is transforming the way we approach development tasks. AI tools are becoming an essential part of the developer's toolkit. Whether it's automating mundane tasks like writing commit messages, creating automation scripts, or even building in-house solutions for code bookkeeping, AI is here to help. You can use AI to create systems that track and manage your codebase efficiently, eliminating repetitive tasks and allowing you to focus on more creative and impactful work.

The key takeaway is that, in order to thrive as a developer, you must embrace the mindset of continuous learning. Don't shy away from experimenting with new tools and technologies. Harness the power of AI and integrate it into your workflow to stay ahead of the curve and continue delivering high-quality, maintainable code.

Next steps for readers

Now that you've gained a solid understanding of code bookkeeping and its importance, the next steps are all about putting these concepts into practice. Don't feel pressured to implement everything at once—take it step by step, starting with the basics and gradually expanding your skill set as you progress in your projects.

The first step is to apply version control to every project you work on, no matter how small. If you're not already using Git, start now. Learn its basics, and get comfortable with tasks like committing changes, branching, and merging. Once you've mastered that, dive deeper into more advanced Git workflows like Gitflow and collaboration features like pull requests and code reviews. These practices will be invaluable as you begin to work with others in the future.

The next step is to introduce testing into your development routine. Start by writing simple unit tests for the code you write, and as you become more comfortable, expand your testing strategy to include integration tests and automated testing tools like Jest or pytest. You can integrate these tests into a CI/CD pipeline as your project grows, ensuring that each change is automatically tested before being deployed.

Finally, embrace automation wherever possible. Start writing scripts to automate repetitive tasks and consider using AI tools to help with code maintenance, commit messages, or even writing basic automation scripts for you. The goal is to continually refine your processes to become more efficient, ensuring that your development workflow becomes smoother and more streamlined over time.

Incorporating these steps into your daily practice will not only help you maintain high-quality code but also set you up for long-term success in your development career. Stay curious, keep learning, and don't be afraid to experiment with new tools and technologies as you grow.

Future of code management

The future of code management is increasingly intertwined with AI-powered tools. As we've discussed throughout this book, automation is the key to reducing repetitive tasks, improving code quality, and enhancing collaboration. With the rise of AI, tools that help manage and automate the bookkeeping process are no longer a luxury—they're becoming an essential part of the developer's ecosystem. From automated commit messages and code reviews to smart refactoring suggestions, AI is already making a profound impact on how we manage our codebases.

Looking ahead, the tools we use to manage code will only become more sophisticated. There is a vast, untapped opportunity in creating solutions that automate the entire code bookkeeping process. The demand for such solutions will only grow as the complexity of software projects increases. So, why not take the opportunity to build and market your own AI-driven tools that can handle these tasks?

As the saying goes in the world of software:

"In the race of a treasure hunt, sell shovels."

In the case of code management, building and offering automation tools for code bookkeeping could be your "shovel." Developers and companies will increasingly look for ways to simplify the process of maintaining, organizing, and tracking their codebase. By creating a solution that takes care of these heavy tasks, you're positioning yourself to meet a critical need in the market.

AI-driven solutions for code management aren't just a trend—they're the future. The more we embrace these tools, the more we'll see their value in streamlining development workflows, enhancing productivity, and ultimately enabling developers to focus on what truly matters: creating innovative, impactful software. Whether you're interested in building such solutions yourself or simply adopting them into your own workflow, it's clear that automation and AI will play a central role in the future of code management.

www.ingramcontent.com/pod-product-compliance
Lightning Source LLC
La Vergne TN
LVHW051242050326
832903LV00028B/2523